Poptart

Poptart

A fresh, frosted sugar rush through
our pre-packaged culture

Liz Langley

Octavo Books

ISBN 0-9673380-0-X

Manufactured in the United States of America
10 9 8 7 6 5 4 3 2 1

For Peter O'Sullivan

vi

Contents

Preface

You can't lie to me. I mean, you could, and I'd probably appreciate it, but while I'm not the sharpest knife in the drawer, I'm not the cheese spreader, either. I know one or two things and one thing I'm sure of is this: If there are a million stories in the Naked City, there are a million beginnings of stories sitting around on disk drives, in spiral notebooks, under the canceled checks in the bottom left-hand drawer of desks. Stories are like romances. Starting them is thrilling. Seeing them through to the end is hard. And as in romance, when the inspiration runs out you convince yourself it will come back one day. Meantime, you go find another distraction.

Everyone who wants to write a book, including me, starts with the preface until they've written more prefaces than they have Christmas cards, failing to realize that without a middle and an end a beginning is just another good intention. We get so jazzed about expounding on why we want to tell the story that we forget about the story. It's like if you go to a dinner party and the host/ess goes on and on about the incredible food they're going to serve, and how they had the mushrooms flown in from the downy hillsides of Squattingthrust, England, and how they skipped "Ally McBeal" for 14 weeks in a row to attend a wine-tasting class so they would know what vintage of Cabernet Voltaire would go with the milk-fed asparagus, and how they had a dominatrix flown in from Germany to personally supervise the trussing of the squabs, and then the kitchen catches fire and burns to a cinder while he or she was busy doing all this PR. That's what prefaces are like. They are much more fun than the actual accomplishing of anything.

Getting all hot and inspired to write a preface for something you haven't done is way more fun than having to write a preface for something that's actually ready to garnish with parsley and shove through the pass-through window, like this book you're about to read 10 minutes at a time in the bathroom. I've spent several years doing a little work at a time to shove these columns through the pass-through windows of the *Orlando Weekly*, the *Toronto Sun* and the *Detroit Metro Times*. Now having done the job, the time for writing a preface has come, and it isn't easy.

What ingredients are supposed to go in a preface?

"I don't know," says my publisher Frank, a person who reads prefaces every day for a living and so ought to know a thing or two about them. It's like asking a kid who eats them all the time what's in a Snickers and having his chocolate, peanut and caramel-smeared face gape back at you in arctic blankness. Finally Frank says, "You tell them what is going to be in the book and why it is a book."

It was like I suddenly turned pee shy. I can write a 500-word freelance piece in my sleep with my brain tied behind my back in a car in a hurricane, and suddenly I had no idea what to say. Crickets chirped. A tumbleweed rolled across the computer screen. Why is this a book, anyway?

To clear my head and get a little perspective on things, I left my apartment in downtown Orlando and headed out to the tourist area of town, a landscape so alien and offensive to most Orlando residents that it makes us feel like Alice pushed through the looking glass.

I drove down Orange Blossom Trail, where one can go to view the hookers in the halting traffic as if they were giraffes and antelopes being gawked at from a Lion Country Safari jeep ("Don't make eye contact with old Tequila or she'll jump right in the car"). I milled around the House of Blues, where an employee recently was murdered and stuffed into a box in a secret third-floor room, and passed the moat that surrounds Planet Hollywood, where a *Newsweek* reporter drowned, drunk, in a couple of feet of water. I drove out to Jungle Land, from which Nala the lioness escaped and eluded captors for several days in the woods. I admired the cheesy old motels and defunct attractions along Highway 192 south of town, attractions like Xanadu, the "home of the future," which was built in the 1970s, looks like a gigantic melted marshmallow with mold growing on it and promised us that in the future we would all have Texas Instruments computers the size of engine blocks sitting on our desks and which didn't have a working bathroom inside the facility, but which had an outhouse of the future that worked just fine.

In the 10 or so days I spent thinking about why the most important inanimate thing in my life was so damn important, I did some other stuff closer to home. I visited a spiritualist museum in Bithlo, a grease spot of a town where the residents are as rusted out and immobile as their trailers, attended a Wiccan celebration of the winter solstice, discussed gunplay at a goth club and discovered the club was the only thing that died, watched my 3-year-old niece bolt down a snootful of wine thinking it was Coke, pretended to live in the Disney-run town of Celebration, closed down the Go! Lounge, closed the Sapphire Supper Club, closed Johnny's Rockin' Bistro and closed the Claddaugh Cottage, where I met a guy named Chuckles who had a Celtic tattoo on his bald head and was missing a few fingers. It was a good time.

And in doing this tremendous amount of stuff in some of the most theatrical and bizarre locales anywhere I concluded the reason why this book is a book is because somewhere along the line I was bored. Orlando is a really strange place in that so many people sit here in one of the world's most sensuous climates, in places that are either beautiful or welcoming or so outrageously horrible that they make conversational subjects for days, and crab about how they hate it here because there's nothing to do. So they make up things to do and they usually turn out not half bad. In all of their desires to make this place more like someplace else, they keep creating reasons for people like me to stay and enjoy it. I just sit in front of my computer finding strange things to write about and enjoy the hell out of writing about them so I can go out and find some more to write about. And while not all of these pieces are Orlando-centered, their point-of-view comes from spending so much time in this strange, fitful, frustrated, snickering, dressed-up, messed-up, screw-it-let's-get-a-beer community. I could have moved away and had a career of Significance, doing Important stuff that would Matter, but I stayed for the bread and circus and woke up with the hangover of a lifetime and plenty of stuff to talk about in the locker room. It's been all right.

And I can't talk about why this is a book without talking about the highest high point of my scribbling career, one which is pure Orlando and which, while the awards, letters and acknowledgements are always great, will always be greater, at least until I start getting fan mail from prison.

It was 1994. It was so bright outside it was like walking into a 7-11 after sitting for hours in a dark bar, a 7-11 with cops in it. And hot, too. This doesn't tell you what season it was. This is Central Florida and saying "it was hot and sunny" could mean it happened on the Fourth of July or Christmas. The event was Fiesta in the Park, a craft fair at which people who make reindeer out of clothespins and knit Florida State garbage can cozies come to exhibit their talents, such as they are. This is what the *Orlando Weekly* inexplicably picked as a good venue for an alternative newsweekly to get its message across, with the kind of reasoning that makes you look at certain people on the street and wonder if they have a mirror in their house. The fiesta is held around Lake Eola, the downtown centerpiece which, I should mention, has a giant fountain right in the middle that looks like a lime Jell-O mold. (Did you know that Salt Lake City, Utah, consumes more lime Jell-O than anywhere else in the world? I'm not sure what that tells you, but it's Jell-O trivia and that is enough.) The water in this lake is so blue-green on some days you'd swear Disney made it, and why not? They own the bandshell.

Anyway, I was supposed to stand in the booth for a certain number of hours to sign autographs and because I get stage fright, my friend Brad and I decided to go to the old Monkey Bar at the Harley Hotel across the street and have a hi-ball before interacting with strangers. The Monkey Bar is a place where you can still hear bands whose names end with "combo" and where you can still see guys who look like tango teachers dance with women who look like Barbara Bush and who look like they're having such a good time an orgy might break out on the buffet tables. It's much quieter than that at 11 A.M., when we walked in, but I'm just saying.

When we left the Harley to find a short line of people waiting for me at the booth, we also found that people from the *Weekly* had put up signs saying I would be giving away orange juice. Since the signs said "Free OJ" at a time when the world's most homicidal golfer was still on trial for murder, we looked like a bunch of radical nitwits. But that wasn't the high point. The high point came when, after speaking to a few people, I was approached by a contingent of guys, guys who looked as though they were about 50 but were probably only 35, guys who looked like they fell out of a vacuum cleaner bag, guys who looked like

ZZ Top without the money and guitars. There are a lot of these guys hanging around Lake Eola, guys whose odor you can actually feel when they pass you, whose beards have yellowed like that part of the molding hit by the sun every day since 1948, sunken-in guys who spend so much time boozing you have to wonder when they do anything that's the kind of stuff you talk about when you're boozing. These guys came up to me and asked for my autograph and said things like, "We love your stuff. We read you all the time. And I think you hang out at some of the same places we do."

And they were right.

Don't get me wrong. I'm happy that anyone in the whole world likes my stuff and am bewildered with joy that I get to do this for a living, a job where I never have to wear pantyhose or feel relieved to get a break from the phones so I can stand around someone's desk eating birthday cake. But the fact that whatever I said gave those guys something to laugh about is something I will never forget even if I ever drink as much as they do.

One last thing I would like to say is that this is not a vanity press book. For those of you lucky enough to never have been interested in writing, a vanity press book is one you pay to have published. I didn't draw a turtle from a matchbook cover to get this thing out, nor did I send in an essay to the Junior Journalists starter club along with a check for $400 in order to get something between these covers. I did stuff that was a lot more debasing than that.

And I hope that from time to time I'll get more going on between the covers than a lot of words.

Little Amish Crackhead

W hen it comes to discerning cultural backgrounds, Americans aren't the sharpest knives in the drawer. We can't even tell people apart who are from here. For example, we're hard pressed to differentiate between the Amish, the Shakers and the Quakers. Now we can, because we know the Amish are the ones with the coke.

The arrest of two Amish men for dealing cocaine for a bike gang (the Pagans, fer god sake) hit "the outside world" with a one-two punch. At first it sounded like either a really bad Charlie's Angels episode (with Farrah undercover as a bra-less milkmaid) or a really good drama (starring Ethan Hawke as the little Amish crackhead and Robert Duvall as the implacable father he's rebelling against). But after our sneering surprise we reacted like a jaded, older brother who found out his younger, naive, sibling had gone bad: "It's okay for me to screw up, I can handle it, you're just a kid, why would you want to wreck your life?"

After all, we like this funny looking kid. The Amish have the cojones to live like they want and not give a damn what we think. You have to respect people who don't care about your opinion. They do their religious thing and never knock on our door asking if we've found Jesus (like they were looking for his house). They're picturesque. We want to drive our minivans into their farms and treat their lives like a tourist attraction, then return to our shallow, glossy world thinking we've done something really earthy. You'd think they'd look at us and get the same view they do from the buggy driver's seat: a bunch of horses asses.

And then we find out MC Daddy Ezekiel and Heavy Jebediah are standing on the corner with actual shovels hanging around their necks, saying:

"Brother Erastus, that 8-ball thou sold me last evensong was crap,"

"Oh yeah? F—— thee."

No wonder those people can raise a barn without machinery. They're wired out of their skulls. That's why they have beards but no mustaches, which would catch any tell-tale white residue. The whole community probably started out with one charismatic Hoover Upright who said at a party "I love all of thee so much, no really I mean it, I really love each and every one of thee. Let's get a big place and all live together." And there they are.

And now that they've found their way to Bolivia, it's only a matter of time before they start doing other big idiot things that we do. When you think you're going to spend the rest of your life with your head in a bonnet making shoofly pie with women named Ruth and Sarah who look like the Smith Brothers, even our worst stuff starts to look good. Before you know it, they're going to have their own Jeremiah Springer show ("That ho stole my hoe. . . ."), their own soap operas ("The Shunned and the Restless"), their own bike gangs (Heck's Angels), buggy jackings, extreme quilting, Beanie Bibles, monster buggy rallies, hostile elders, wet bonnet contests, the sheep and cow fetishists support group, their own website (made of wood), transvestism (wherein Amish women secretly wear one of those Abe Lincoln beards and parade around in front of the mirror when no one is about), and will start going to public schools so they can bring guns there like everyone else. See what happens when you name a town "Intercourse"?

Okay, as that older brother, it's our responsibility to tease and torment the younger sibling within an inch of its life, but it's not a nice thing to do, especially because they are kind of sensitive. Case in point: A wire story noted that an Amish cherry farmer asked the reporter whether the outside world was disappointed in them over the arrests. It is important, another offered, for them to set a good example. It was as though we gave them some firecrackers and they were afraid we'd be mad at them for blowing their own fingers off.

This is why we like this little sibling better than the other extremists our motherland spawns like kudzu. They really mean what they say. It's hard to believe that they're perfect, but it's also kind of painful to think that our cheap way of dealing with things is undermining theirs.

So maybe this incident is a little eye-opener for both sides, a little chance to do some more growing up for the older one that didn't set such a great example and the little one that followed it anyway. If they dealt a little more realistically with the uncomfortable problems their teenagers are facing, their troubles may not have gotten this far. And if we practiced a little of the fortitude and contemplation we claim to admire so wistfully every time they are the subject of a PBS documentary, we could simplify our lives a little and not have to feel like the bad example all the time. After all, when siblings start to get a little older, they start realizing they have more in common than they thought.

And the first thing we ought to do for our brothers is get them some phones up there. That way we can call them and ask them if they can hook us up with some pot. Aside from trying to set a better example, teasing unmercifully is just one of those things, as older brothers, we feel obligated to do.

Leading men

Between felonious preachers and clinic bombers I sometimes swear off religious items like a wino throwing his hip nip into the sewer.

But a drunk always finds his way back to the liquor store.

The sign in the Booze Barn window this time said "Wives, submit graciously to your husbands," a Bible passage that the Southern Baptist convention made a declaration, meaning wives should always defer to their husbands as leaders of the household. Defenders say it's God's call for leadership within the family (which one pastor compared to running a Wal-Mart) and that the man's part is harder because he has to lead.

The notion that men should head the parade because they have a built-in baton is something people in the '90s are about as likely to buy as a butter churn and assumes that all men are Solomon and Lincoln, when a great many are Beavis and Butthead. It should make women laugh. Instead, it makes us freak like we got a roach in our hair.

The following could lead to a reason . . . if you don't mind following a girl.

This guy I don't really know pulls my hips towards his, saying "Give yourself to me." Or maybe "Give it up to me." I forget. The blood rushed out of my head like it had a train to catch. "Spread your legs," he says offhandedly, like baggers say "paper or plastic."

"Buy me a drink first?" I ask. Caught off guard, he puts his hand over his eyes and laughs, like the overtones of these words, that he must say to women often, never dawned on him until now.

Tango teachers say these things all the time, and that's what Tony Benchoff from TC Dance Studios is doing, teaching me and my colleague to dance, something we want to know since the Swing craze has hit Orlando like a hard rain ought to. Swing is very '90s: interactive and user-friendly. You have to dance with someone, not near them. The classes are fun and get progressively easier, but early on I have a problem with leading. I want to.

"Don't pull him," says Tony, stopping me from dragging my luckless partner around like a bag of laundry. "He leads. The man always leads." Normally I'd get in a big Ms. Magazine wad over this kind of talk, but I like Tony. He's chatty, casual, has shown us how to cha-cha to rap and is an excellent dancer who I'm paying to learn from. But I secretly think "Why shouldn't I pull him? I think I know where to go, shouldn't I lead, even if I'm a girl?"

The answer is no; submit graciously. I'm demoted because someone slipped me the wrong set of chromosomes. "The man's part is actually harder because he has to lead," Tony says.

Before his students descend to a level of physical comedy associated with Shemp, Tony intervenes to show how this benign dictatorship works. And the damnedest thing happens. When he leads . . . I follow. Like a kid after an ice cream truck. Normal feet have appeared where my two left ones were and they're doing steps I've only seen on TV. "How come you can do all that?" says my equally bewildered colleague. Beats me, but if Tony danced off a cliff I'd think "Hell, he knows what he's doing. See ya suckers," and follow him. Blind faith kicks ass.

But I can afford to be blind. I'm not being lead by the blind. I'm being lead by a pro who projects the kind of confidence that comes from a great deal of training, like a pilot can get a plane to go where he wants, whereas a novice might crash it right into the airport. To show that men can lead badly, he dances listlessly, which is frustrating, then arrogantly, which makes me feel like a bass on a 12-gauge hook. It's not the gender of the leader (if it was, women couldn't teach men to lead in dance), but their character that can make the dance a dream or a dud.

And the only reason I can follow is not because he's a man, but because he's deferring to me being at a beginner's level, and not using the full range of talent he could display with a woman who is an equal partner.

Life isn't as smooth as a dance floor and it doesn't have pre-set steps you could learn from a pro, or everybody would. But relationships are a dance, a union, not an army that needs a leader or a Wal-Mart that needs a CEO. Women shouldn't be told to defer to their men anymore than you would ask one dancer to be a little less graceful and passionate so the other one can shine. Diminishing one disables both. Like love, dance only looks simple, a lot of sweat and mutual effort went into it that you didn't see. And good luck in the genital lotto may make you think you're a leader, but it doesn't automatically make you one anyone would want to follow.

And in dance, it isn't the woman clinging to the man but her pushing away from him slightly that gives them stability, a use of her strength that makes a union move forward as one elegant being.

Still, I have found that automatic male leadership can be a dazzling thing. Provided it's strictly ballroom.

Around the world
in 80 drinks

Those wine people, you gotta hand it to 'em. In fact you gotta hand it to 'em every two minutes, if you don't leave the bottle at the table.

Honestly, they're the Trekkies of the drinking set, so deep into their habit that they come up with more terminology than Dickens to describe a glass of grape juice. Most times, when you overhear someone describe something as "balanced but flat," "tart with legs" or "yeasty, harsh and gassy," they might well be describing their date from the previous night. It turns out they also could be using bona fide terms to describe their wine.

We hadn't given the matter much thought until a recent dinner at a swank restaurant in Canada (not, like, at Epcot; the actual country) and our waiter praised our wine choice, saying it was "fat and round, not dry and crispy."

"Fat and round." Say it—it feels good, sweet and rich, rolling around in your mouth like a couple of

Milk Duds. Fat and round. We said it, repeatedly puzzling over how a drink could be described as such. Say "fat and round," wrapping your mouth around those vowels as if it was the Venus de Willendorf of wine, fat enough to need an extra seat on a plane and round enough to make a shady man hide his wedding ring. Now say "dry and crispy," like it's some old hag wine that has to pay you to pick it up. The best thing about this patter is that when someone says something ridiculous, which they will after a few glasses, you get to look at them and say, "You and your fat, round wine."

Grape expectations

With the vineyards in some of the more rural, hillbilly redneck parts of the state, Florida may eventually become known as wine country, the Nappy Valley perhaps. Laugh now, but one day we could take over ABC shelves clear across the country with Orange Blossom Blanc and Cou Rouge (red neck).

And then there's Disney. While they don't have their own Snow White Zinfandel or Pinot Chio, the mecca of family entertainment is just now paying homage to pleasures of the flesh—at least the flesh with tastebuds on it—during Epcot's International Food and Wine Festival, which has become a fall tradition.

Normally we don't get to trumpet much about Disney, because normally they yank us back by the collar when we attempt to sneak in through the employee exits. This week, however, we joined our fellow professional journalists (*you* know I'm not qualified and *I* know I'm not qualified, but *they* don't know that so keep your mouth shut) for the start of Disney World's 25th anniversary party. While the rest of the country squinted over Iraq, welfare reform and kids bringing guns to school, the big question we faced at Disney was whether the castle looked better in gray or as a hot-pink birthday cake. I vote cake, but then I believe I wrote in "cake" in recent elections for school board, county commission and Senate.

The object of Epcot's Food and Wine Festival is to move around the World Showcase sampling food and wine from different countries—even some Epcot hasn't recognized with a pavilion—for $1 or $2 a pop. We all know how to play Drinking Around the World at Epcot—you go in, speed past all the educational stuff and embark on your world tour starting in Canada, where you stand there saying, "I can't believe they don't sell beer in Canada," wander off to England, start drinking and putter your way around the pretend globe, becoming more of a charming, affable diplomat along the way until you finally get to Mexico, where you poke someone in the shoulder, say "I'm gonna tell you shumpin," and fall ass-over-tea-kettle into a family from Chicago. It's a great game. But the festival is greater.

Whine not

"But," you say, "I have no knowledge of wines and all this vintening would be wasted on me." You don't know anything about cars either, but you drive. My wine knowledge is limited to choosing a color that goes with my outfit (I spill a lot), but I had a blast. For example, I can now tell you that there is a wine in New Zealand that you can use as a nail polish remover. I know that it doesn't matter whether the cider you get in England is sweet or dry, it's all equally fabulous and explains how they put up with that weather. I can tell you the main question in the Spanish Inquisition probably was, "Where do they have better wine than here?" and that they did all that exploring in search of better drinks. I can tell you that it's not math and zen but plum wine and sushi that make the Japanese superior. I can tell you the reason the Germans don't start a war every year is that their beer is good enough to keep even them relaxed. But I can't tell you why the band in Norway was playing "Tequila." They must have gotten to that cider.

Anyway, go widen your world and your hips. Wining and dining in this style beats whining and dining at home any day.

Baked, bony and terrified

Why it's no fun being a rich lady in Lauderdale

There are more rich people in South Florida by the power of a million than there are in Central Florida," says Mike, who is rich. We are standing in Mike and Pat's kitchen in their canal-side home in Lauderdale. There are more canals in Fort Lauderdale than there are in Venice, and on this one there are yachts parked at every dock.

There are a lot of people who automatically dislike and distrust people with money. This is how richbastard got to be one word. It's folkloric thinking. The villain of the story is never poor. It's always some rich bastard—Ebeneezer Scrooge, Mr. Potter, Veruca Salt—that makes everybody else in the story miserable. And when we see their kindred in real life—the Ferdinand and Imeldas, the Jim and Tammys—it confirms our worst fears, that the rich are out to build their castles on our broken bones.

I don't have this problem with rich people. Other people's wealth is like music. You might not even be able to make it yourself, but it's good that someone else can and you can enjoy it. And it could inspire you to make your own.

Standing on the canal in Lauderdale, it's all I can do not to let the dough I'm looking at blend with some kind of admirational yeast and come volcanoing out of me with some brilliant observation like, "Garsh, yer loaded, aincha? How do I get loaded?" (I already know the answer: You work half days. Either the first 12 hours or the second.) So we decided to get the other kind of loaded and went to Las Olas.

Most every town has at least one fashionable street with bright, trendy boutiques and sleek bar/restaurants with tiny white lights. In Lauderdale, Las Olas is that place.

Not every town is so wealthy that the flyers on the tables advertise a local store where you can get "yacht provisions," like they did at Bar Amici. Still, the place didn't have the kind of clenched-jaw, country club, Who's Who, Be My C.Z. Guest atmosphere one fears of the rich. There was football on TV. We sat at a high-up table, settled in with a couple of Stoli Oranjs and began to drink in the ambient privilege like a couple of split ends soaking on a placenta pack. We needed this.

They say the rich are different from you and me, but there were some noticeable differences among the rich themselves, mainly between the men and the women.

The men were relaxed, from the retirees who sat at the high tables and ordered rounds of beer, to the

14

youngish professor type who came for dinner with his wife, daughter and three of her girlfriends. The men were all George Hamil-tanned, and they all looked about as tense as a bowl of pudding.

Calm. Composed. Cool. All these C-adjectives and probably more. Clever, Credible, Crafty—that's what these guys were. This Confidence is the best thing money can do for you, the Clout, Connections and Cash to come out smelling like Clean sheets, no matter where you've been.

Some of the women were dressed like this, but most were shrink-wrapped in the tightest black dresses you ever saw, tourniquet dresses, and had to walk in those little geisha hops you take when you're trying on shoes that are lashed together with nylon. They had on enough gold jewelry to sink a helium balloon, enough hairspray to keep the Black Forest still in a headwind. And their makeup—my parents' house has less paint on it.

We've all heard that money can't buy happiness, and watching a difference like this makes you wonder if it's true. Those guys were content and probably would have been if they were just Average Joe instead of Richard Corey. And the women just made you wonder how anyone could have that kind of money and look so tired and skittish. Don't they get to pay someone to be tired and skittish for them?

Not if what's causing the exhaustion and nerves is within and all your doing to fix it is without. Like this fascinating woman we saw in The Floridian, a

24-hour diner on Las Olas, a mix of the trendy (stainless steel riveted counter) and the campy (Christmas garlands everywhere).

"Late night last night?" the waitress said when we all asked for very large glasses of water and very speedy cups of coffee. "I know. I usually just keep a big pitcher by my bed," she said, her empathy fake, you could tell. This was a girl you could smoke cigarettes with.

Anyway, we sat in The Floridian and had exactly the kind of customized breakfast you want after a long night. Then I spotted her, eating her cantaloupe and yolkless omelette in the seat directly behind us.

She had had more surgeries than I'm sure she could recall, enough surgeries to turn a dog into a cat. Her eyes were almost on the sides of her head, like a fish, but were wide and pretty in their weird way, her skin so fragile, like the silky-smooth wet wax of a burning candle.

It stopped there. Her neck looked like a pork rind.

Her body had been aerobicized into longevity, which you might be able to tell by looking at it, but you didn't get a chance. She could have done a million butt crunches or ab fabs or whatever, but she didn't need to because her "I work out" clothes—bike pants, leotard—announced it for her.

Her catlike eyes and blonde hair gave her that Barbara Edenish quality that no age can put asunder. She was Ozymandias, baked to a crisp by the Florida sun.

While I looked over at her, thinking what it must be like to be a surgery slave, wondering if her life was empty and if she was empty enough to not know it, she was probably looking at me thinking how sad it was to see such dark-lidded, puffy alcoholic dissipation in one so young, and how I probably didn't need to eat all my toast. You say tomato.

Baptist boycott inspires
a turn for the verse

Every year for the past few the Southern Baptist convention has found a reason to boycott Disney and though every year the boycott is thoroughly ineffectual and Disney keeps growing, like the Blob, every day. Still, every year the issue of the Baptist boycott is one very much discussed in Orlando, likely because everyone is wondering what kind of kooks could see "The Lion King" as evil? I tried to find out by becoming one.

This thing between Disney and the Baptists is kind of like having to choose sides between "Benny Hill" and "Hee Haw," isn't it? It's just that silly.

The Baptists are mad because Disney extended health benefits to the partners of its gay employees. Now, it's only fair that anyone, straight or gay, who marries should be compensated in some manner financially. It makes up for the time when, in a few years, they look over on the couch and think, "God, I'm chained to that lemon."

And most of Disney's employees are gay. Come on. You don't think straight men could be tirelessly tidy, peppy, well-groomed and listen to "Little Mermaid" all day, do you?

Now, on the other hand you have the Baptists. One dictionary definition of baptist is "one that baptizes," which certainly wouldn't be such a bad thing. Certainly there is a need for someone to throw water at those who go religious, if only to snap them out of it. But Southern Baptists find less joy in throwing water around than weight. They are threatening to boycott Disney for handing out benefits willy-nilly or willy-nelly, and making movies for grownups.

I'm often irritated by people who snub all tastes that aren't theirs. I'm not only talking about folks who grandstand about their beliefs. It would do the world a world of good if everyone would try on someone else's taste for a week and see what they think. That way, if they ridicule it, at least they can back up their claims.

So I tried to be a boycotting Baptist for two hours:

Day one: Screw up within 10 minutes by reading three daily horoscopes—not only my horoscope, but those of my friends and enemies. I like knowing when my enemies are going to have a really rotten day. For witchcraft and wrath, go back three spaces.

Try reading. This is an easy one. The book I decided to read was the Bible. Do not own a Bible. Library is closed. Go back three spaces for cussing out library.

Find tiny little personal Bible given to me by toadying admirer. Inscribed "Dear Liz. Here are some of my favorite witticisms. Love God." Begin reading and can't help remembering SCTV's Dave Thomas reading of Genesis: "In the beginning, there was nothing. And the Lord said 'Let there be light.' And there was still nothing. But now yez could see it." For snickering at Genesis, go back five spaces.

Ah, there's the rub

Day Two: Go to Baptists for insight. Attempt to cruise hunky Baptist boy browsing in T-shirt section of religious bookstore. Figure there must be frequent-fire miles straight to hell for this one. Go back eleven spaces. Consider slipping him note that says "I'd like to fellowship you." Go back 47,000 spaces for laughing.

Read "Bible Flip Answers," an easy-to-read chart about New Age religions that discusses reincarnation, Higher Consciousness "and other trendy stuff." Part about "Witnessing," says, "Share your testimony; a relationship with an impersonal force is impossible." Clearly whoever wrote this has never owned a "personal massager." Go back 10 spaces for that one.

Day three: Try to imagine treating friends as

second-rate because they are gay. Cannot continue thinking this way. Promise to try to be more intolerant in the future.

Go back 50 spaces for rushing to look for remarks about sex in Baptist books. Find teenage book called *Sex, What's That?* by Susan Lanford. Girls ask about their periods, boys ask about wet dreams and are treated to a discussion of masturbation. "You were curious about your body. To rub your penis felt good." Go back 150 spaces for wondering what they suggest you do when you don't have a penis of your own to rub and have to find someone else's. Find it curious that girls don't have any masturbatory information and think that Lanford thinks that girls just never consider it. Go back 100 spaces for knowing that's not true.

Listen to Jesus station on car radio. Listen to guy on radio say "Gawd." Get annoyed by all this kissing up. Think what it would be like to really believe that the whole world was like a big rec room and we were just kids and Jesus was the rec supervisor. Have a moment of contentment thinking we are all just kids. Go forward two spaces. Think how some of these kids never learned how to drive and you'd like to smash them right into a nearby light pole. Go back two spaces. Remember we aren't just kids anymore, we are grown-ups who have to try to tolerate each other, even the bad drivers, the Disney executives and the Baptists. Go back four spaces in Baptist game.

Continue to hold own in personal playground.

In all I went back 47,332 spaces and forward three trying to be a good Baptist. I know they are just "trying to put the God back into everyday living." How about "My God, just mind your own business?"

Barbie's emotional makeover

If you really wanted to kick a woman in the self-esteem there is no more pejorative thing to call her than a Barbie Doll. It implies that she's a shallow, insipid puppet and one word that defined America's worst suspicions about itself, plastic. It meant she didn't have much more use than the doll itself: You can change her outfits, and then what?

So in recent years, Barbie has done something eerily human. She has realized she can no longer get by on her looks and has gotten an interior facelift.

She has become a doctor, a business woman and acquired such a huge circle of ethnic cohorts she makes the UN look shy. The possibilities for Barbies of different lifestyles were as endless as they were in real people. We waited for Trailer Trash Barbie (comes with Elvis poster, bottle of VO and two kids who live with their grandma), Saint Barbie (prays a lot, shuns Ken, can do parlor tricks), Litigious Barbie (she'll sue anyone) and the Barbie Crack House (no furniture, broken pipes, but Barbie don't care). It never went that far. Barbie being a doctor and an Eskimo was about all the reach she would get.

And while Barbie herself stays above natural law, she does have a disabled friend, Share a Smile Becky, who comes with her own hot pink wheelchair.

Make all the snarky remarks you like, but Becky could well be very satisfying for little girls who, due to injury or illness, can't get around like their friends can. And hot pink is a nice touch. Hell, why not use the parallel universe of Barbie to help kids be more at ease with lots of different kinds of people? We could be ushering in a generation of children who are nicer than we were and in 50 years the axiom "Kids can be cruel" could be obsolete.

Then again, it's also possible that children will tamper with Becky's brakes. Kids can be cruel.

But already there's a glitch in Becky's busy schedule of slumber parties and weekends at the beach. Her wheelchair doesn't fit in the elevator of the Barbie Dream House. She can go to the Barbie Travelling Surprise House but can't get upstairs in the Dream House. Mattel has received complaints about the lack of accessibility and will soon introduce Barbie Folding Pretty House with a wider front door and no stairs. Basically, Becky came out with the intention of including the disabled as the same and, through one glaring oversight, showed she was different. As though difference is the worst thing that could ever happen to a girl.

Don't even try resolving this problem because this is how you'll sound: So why can't Ken just carry Becky into the elevator? I mean, the wheelchair probably folds up or dismantles, right? Unless it's a question of Becky getting around the house by herself, which it shouldn't be, because it isn't her house, it's Barbie's house and what's she doing there alone anyhow?

Unless she's house-sitting, and then, you'd think as a doctor, Barbie would be more sensitive to the Dream House's Old World design flaws. She's got a zillion international friends, fercrissake, why can't Skipper housesit?

Before you start thinking about whether the ACLU will represent Becky in a suit against the original Dream House contractor, try to remember: They're dolls. Becky can actually get to the upper floor. We appreciate the real need for real disabled people to have independent access. We appreciate the irony that politically correct architecture is coming to Barbie's world and ours at the same rate. And yet if you really wanted to take the situation literally, Becky isn't alone. In real life, not a whole lot of people have access to the Dream House.

You'll never see Old Barbie in the Dream House either, Becky, ditto Stroke Barbie, Weirdo Leftist Intellectual Barbie, Midlife Crisis Barbie, Fat Barbie, Just Kind of Average Barbie or even real Barbie.

In real life the dream house would be filled with older white men. Barbie might be one of their dates or the caterer, if you were going to take things literally and keep them in the real, non-accessible world.

But no child would likely be literal enough to leave Becky; sitting by the elevator because she wouldn't fit into it. They'd just put her on the top where she belongs. They can't really see limitations until they start getting told about them. Thankfully, playthings represent what can be if you keep your mind and imagination from getting handicapped, which happens all too quickly.

And anyhow, when you think about it literally, Barbie herself does not actually walk into the elevator. She cannot get in there by herself either.

The Giant Hand controls her. It puts Barbie in the elevator and can fly Becky upstairs. Or it can put both of them in the dog's bowl. It could make Becky Queen of Everything while Barbie has her head pulled off in a freak blow-drying accident. Just as invisible forces push real people into painful or ecstatic fates, the Giant Hand of a child decides who gets to Barbie's top floor. The Giant Hand cares not for "should be." The Giant Hand just acts. And that's a definite parallel between Barbie's world and our own.

And there's no reason for Barbie to get a whole new house. Why can't they just invite Lesbian Barbie over and have her show them how to modify the damn chair or make their own chair that fits? Then they can all have pizza and Cokes from a penthouse view and celebrate their defeat of the male-dominated medical-industrial complex. See? This Barbie thing can be fun after all.

Monkey see,
monkey screw

If you don't remember Ciccolina it's because you never saw her. A giantess with ass-length platinum hair, usually adorned with a crown of flowers, Ciccolina was a member of the Italian Parliament whose prior career was porn actress. She had deeply held political beliefs such as "War I no like; Nude, I like." She offered to have sex with Saddam Hussein if he would get out of Iraq. It didn't work, but think about solving international conflict with bomb shells instead of bombs. It's just so . . . Austin Powers.

From the once-beautified floor of the Italian government we go deep into the jungle of Zaire and a species of ape that thinks pretty much along the same lines as Ciccolina. Bonobos are so like chimps they were thought to be the same species until primatologists noticed some gaps. Bonobos are more delicate, make different sounds and, unlike the chimps, they rarely fight, don't brandish weapons or commit infanticide. And they have sex all the time. Just all the time. They do it to procreate, to relax, to appease, to celebrate, in every possible combination and by themselves.

Bonobos are the Sex Addicts Anonymous of the animal world. They also share 98% of our DNA.

Now don't lie—whether it's Monica Lewinsky's ability to identify the president's penis in a line-up or gossip about your friends, sex is always cock of the walk as far as entertaining subjects. And the Club Med lifestyle of the bonobo is damn entertaining. But according to an in-depth book, *Bonobo: The Forgotten Ape*, by Frans de Waal and Frans Lanting, there's a great deal more to them that's important to us, aside from just another creature whose lifestyle we can see on television and envy.

The most curious point about bonobos concerns their place in evolution, a theory we'll assume you buy into. If you don't, if you think instead that God was bored and unfulfilled and wanted something to love so he made some people—in other words, we're here because God was thinking along the same line as the pregnant 14-year-olds on Springer—this stuff won't interest you.

Humans, bonobos and chimps share a common lineage, but, for lots of reasons, bonobos went unnoticed and chimps, who also share 98% of our DNA were considered our closest relatives. Chimps are loud, violent, aggressive and beat up on their own kind, make tools, live in male-dominated societies, are political and have a sense of self-awareness like we do. Also, back in 1925 a "crucial missing link" fossil was found and decided to be a blood thirsty monster. These theories were popularized around the times of the World Wars when people were seeing the most abysmally violent traits of their species, making it easy to believe it was in their genes to be brutal and cruel. The self-image seemed to stick.

Then, out of the closet and into the street, here comes the kindred bonobo. They have female-dominated societies, are largely uncompetitive and non-violent and exhibit high intelligence but not through tool use. Their intellect comes out in their sympathy and empathy—anticipating what their pals are feeling and acting accordingly, which contributes to bonding, enhances group strength and safety and keeps the peace, things we do as well, but which didn't go into the hopper of self-image like the violence of chimps did.

If you haven't seen anything but the Three Stooges, it's hard to imagine how your taste and style would have been different if you had been exposed to Woody Allen. If we had been able to see the cooperation, free sexuality, female-leading and general serenity of the bonobos and identify it as a trait within ourselves alongside the war-mongering, inventiveness and male dominance of chimps, it's hard to imagine how differently we would have viewed our past and thus handled our future. In light of these new-found relations, one theory that suggests itself is that in the genetic jambalaya some of us got more chimp and some of us got more bonobo. You see the guy screeching himself into heart attack country at his kid at a little league game, to the detriment of the other kids and antagonism of the group as a whole, but who can fix your air-conditioner when it's broken, that one is full of chimp. You see a guy who can't work a tire gauge but can smooth-talk his way into getting someone else to, is pleasant to be around, easy to talk to and sees relationships as matters of fun and love and not just power plays, that one got a lot of bonobo. Most people are probably a combination, but if you look hard, you can see which side of the jungle you lean toward.

Personally, I envy the bonobos and wish we had known about them earlier so we could have adhered a bit more closely to their standard of living. All they do is eat, sleep and screw around all day and the women control the food. If people lived more like this fewer things would get done, but we'd all be so relaxed who would care? According to the authors, Pacific Islanders were a very highly sexualized people until Victorian society came and brought them morals . . . and venereal disease. They, maybe we all, would have been better off if they had told them to go screw themselves.

Cool doesn't count
if it requires a sweat

It's sad enough that TV is so integral to my life that I took all the channels I could get like an alcoholic gargling down a bottle of nail polish remover. What's sadder is that now, possessed of The Learning Channel, Discovery and A&E, the only televised journey I've taken into history has been through Nick-at-Night and Nick's TV Land.

Is it so wrong to skip the History Channel's "The War Years," "The Century of War" and "The Vietnam War?" The TV Land variety show lineup offered an equally valuable and multilayered history lesson, especially viewed with hindsight. Remember the News of the Future segment on "Laugh-In"? The phrase "President Ronald Reagan" got an enormous laugh in 1969. Still does, at parties.

But the ultimate time-space mirror was seeing Dean Martin, the definitive conduit through which we were fed the 1960s. Not The '60s, the 1960s. I've said it before and, since retro is so damn popular, I'll say it again. There were two versions of that era. The '60s was that ragged, sign-carrying, drug-bingeing, beat-poetry (to death in some cases), "kill your parents" time that dragged consciousness and unconsciousness to heights no one had ever seen before.

The 1960s was populated primarily by the parents it was suggested one kill. The 1960s was the martini swilling, cigarette smoking, wise-cracking, sex-mongering height of breezy charm, when being socially conscious meant seeing to it that nobody's glass was empty. You smiled and took yourself lightly and that was all that mattered.

Straight up

Like any other kid allowed to stay up that late, I watched "The Dean Martin Show" when I was 6 and was as transfixed as anyone at the Ascension might have been. Everyone was witty, well-dressed, graceful and glib. And then there were the girls, the Golddiggers, Dean Martin's entourage of statuesque beauties, all 9-feet-tall, 38-24-36, with gorgeous clothes and Niagara Falls of hair, so luxurious you could hang onto it and repel off them, if that was your idea of a good time.

Given the endless debate about how TV influences kids (mix one shot snoring with two shots yawn), reviewing "The Dean Martin Show" was a real eye-opener. The guy was adorably blasted all the time, and it didn't look like an act. More to the point, it was encouraged, and by the network. Back then

Schaeffer was advertised as "the beer to have when you're having more than one." Not to mention the fact that Martin smoked constantly, especially while singing. And "Golddiggers." Imagine anyone getting away with naming a group of ornamental women Golddiggers today. I aspired to be a Golddigger as a kid, too. But the most golddigging I ever got around to occurred only when I got some popcorn stuck between a couple of fillings. There just turned out to be other things to do.

Now the retro swinger thing is making a comeback. Sadly, it's doing so with all the clumsiness of a drunk trying to corner you for a kiss. Don't get me wrong. I do love the whole Dino, martini, cocktail scene . . . of the 1960s. But the ham-handedness with which happy-hour revisionists are attempting it is something of an insult to the ease and calm good humor it's supposed to invoke. They look like they're trying too hard. Consider the magazine we saw a few days ago, Milton, with a sepia photo of Mr. Berle on the cover, tag-line, "We drink. We smoke. We gamble." Why not just say, "We are so hip it hurts," or any other sentiment that an odd, greasy teenager would scribble into his notebook with a ballpoint?

On the rocks

No, the real lovers of the genre know the cocktail hour, the quiet drink, the silk-light music of the Sinatra boxset, the sweet, stolen flirt are all pleasures of the spirit and can't be dictated or deconstructed any more than the perfect kiss. Those moments, and they are moments, not ways of life, are quantum and Zen. Try to force it and it will shrink like a man intimidated. Try to capture it and it will escape giggling, like a girl who has had enough of you and not enough of the party.

Loving an era is one thing, but trying to resuscitate it is like trying to bring back an old romance, tingly at first but in the end contrived, awkward and thuddingly disappointing. Let's just hope there aren't any more deeply buried eras that someone tries to bring back. Everyone might end up wearing Ascots, having butlers, snorting snuff, speaking in horribly affected English accents and quoting Oscar Wilde. Now there was a man who knew how to drink like a grownup. And he knew then what all the revisionists have forgotten. That absinthe makes the heart grow fonder. Oh, and the importance of being a little less earnest.

Covenant marriage

When you think of things that come out of Louisiana, you might think of voodoo swamp witches, low high school reading scores, unzipped politicians, and tourists draped in Mardi Gras beads like stewed Christmas trees. If you thought you heard the initial rumblings of an enlightened cultural move, you would tilt your head toward New York or California, not the bayou.

Well, there are little surprises lurking around every corner to prove your jaded, world-weary ass wrong all the time, aren't there? Wonders never cease and Louisiana has shown that it is as adept at looking at things from new angles as a kid with a shoe-mirror. They have legislated a brand new way of getting married.

Louisiana has tried to tame a divorce rate that's growing like kudzu (40% of marriages end in divorce) by going to the root of the problem, marriage. As of August 15, they can go for the traditional, "no-fault" marriage, which is apparently easier to get rid of than *National Geographic*s, or they can get the new kind. Called "a covenant marriage," this would require couples to have extensive premarital counseling (whereas they usually just have extensive premarital sex) and agree to counseling to solve problems during the marriage (instead of the traditional throwing of things). Also, unless one party commits child or spouse abuse, adultery or a felony leading to prison, the wait for a divorce could be up to two years. If your marriage was a burning building, the normal marriage would be a fallen wall at the end of an asbestos hallway whereas the covenant marriage would be a drain pipe on the third floor you might get through if you suck in. Getting out of this one ain't so easy.

Watching Louisiana do this to the rest of the country is kind of like watching some nerdy geek call on a big-mouthed braggart to prove his stories true. Traditional America, in this scenario, is the big dope, the one who doesn't read the directions, chooses a car for its color. This is a country that has adopted "just do it" as a school of serious philosophy, willfully forgetting someone made it up to sell sneakers.

And even the most stoic and thoughtful would want the bright red cherry of fun and love that marriage promises to be our birthright. Even Mr. Spock was married. It's the most endearing institution of all and the most fun to get involved in. Queens, drag or actual, don't even get to dress like brides do. The wedding is the best excuse for the biggest parties anyone ever attends. It's also the only time you get presents for possibly making a huge error. No one said to me, "So, you're majoring in Humanities. Here's a toaster." Then there's the biggest bait of all, the fact that someone else is going to publicly acknowledge that you're the bee's meow, or the cat's knees, or whatever sweet thing they think, and that you're worth being legally stuck with. Marriage is the only time you ever get to do that. If I had a ceremony for every time I'd committed to a friend for better, worse, I'd have enough toasters to make Pop-Tarts for Peru. It's no wonder, after lots of thought, so many people say, "What the hell? Wanna?"

Covenant marriage may be the rattle under the hood that alerts many people to the fact that their thinking on this issue needs an overhaul. And the great thing is, the slacker marriage is still available for those who want it. In fact, just choosing which one you want could be very telling. If you asked a couple, on the count of three, which kind of marriage they wanted, pure gut reaction, and one said "Covenant!" with red-blooded certainty, while the other looked around for emergency exits, you know you've got a problem from jump street and might need to think about this. Children may cause a biological alarm to go off, but you can hit the snooze button on marriage until you're nearly dead.

And considering a choice in marriage styles, like buffalo wings and caller ID, is such a great idea that you have to wonder why no one ever thought of it before. In fact, there should be more than two choices. The marriage menu should look like the beer list at Hubbs. Sam Beher should be there vowing to fit any human. If you wanted something more severe than the Covenant, you could have the Kamikaze marriage, to the death, no exceptions, but you get as many kamikazes a day as needed to make the arrangement bearable. Arthur C. Clarke, one World Wide Webster noted, came up with the idea of the Contract Marriage. The couple would contract to stay together for seven years with an option to renew. This, with a variance in years, is the most sensible idea since the roof. This one could even extend to premarital relationships: "I promise to be your date until, mostly until the sex gets old, after which we will both acknowledge this fact, say "It's not you, it's me," even though we know it's you, and swear to abstain from falsely reporting each other to America's Most Wanted, broadcasting your sexual habits or calling in to cry or hector me at work for a period not to exceed six months, after which all bets are off."

That's the one I'd know about best, since, if you squeezed most of my dates you'd get a pitcher of Country Time and since I've never been married. I have the standard GenX fear of commitment which I'm convinced comes less from watching our parents' marriages than the fact that we've all signed a health club contract and then stopped going after three months. This Ballyophobia teaches a great wariness of letting your enthusiasm run away with you. You keep paying and paying and paying, whether you care anymore or not.

But even though I have been known to buy plastic forks because I can't commit to a flatware pattern, I do know something about sticking with it. There is alchemy that can happen with another person where you find yourself committed without being covetous, showing your concern without stating it, wanting to impress them and never making your criticism personal. This careless caring is simple, unadorned friendship, and if you have that, no contract could bind you more.

And if you don't, get specifics, in writing. It pays to be cynical and if you aren't extremely careful with yourself when it comes to giving your heart and possessions away, the only time you'll be hearing "commitment" again may be before "hearing."

Dress code

Yes, the Bill/Monica romance is old news but the issues of romance are eternal.

Okay, it's finally out. President Clinton admitted he had an inappropriate relationship with Monica Lewinsky. I think that means he had her working on his car. That would be totally inappropriate. She doesn't look like she knows a thing about cars.

A sexual relationship, on the other hand, seems like just the ticket. They had their little fling and the country was prosperous and peaceful. Then Clinton's out of Monica's company for awhile and what happens? Bang, we're bombing the Sudan. See? People are just like champagne bottles; if they get shaken up and aren't allowed to uncork, they will just explode anyway, with messier results.

Some people were disappointed in Bill for not fessing up earlier, indicating that they could have told their sexual history on TV with total impunity, if the glare from their halos didn't blind the cameras. That's terribly sad. Any sex life you could blab about to a daytime TV audience would hardly be worth listening to. If you haven't done anything you want to keep secret, you're not really applying yourself.

Far from being disappointed, I'm more impressed with Clinton than ever. Most guys can barely hold down one mediocre job and get an occasional phone number. This man is smoothly running a huge country and it turns out he's been doing it with one hand tied behind his back, or occupied elsewhere, anyway. One finger on the button and another one up some girl's dress, that is dexterity. And he's made daytime television more interesting than "All My Children" has done in months. People are afraid he will tarnish the image of the office for future generations, but just the opposite will occur. Now when little boys are told "You could be president one day," they're going to see how much action he gets and try 20 times harder than they would have if they only had Ferrett Face Bush or that one that called his wife Mommie (if that isn't an inappropriate relationship, I don't know what is) to look up to.

And with a day planner packed fuller than a Mode model in a one-size-fits-all teddy, are we really supposed to believe this guy picks out his own ties?

In case you've been watching higher quality fashion television than CNN, it's now being speculated that Bill wore a busy-but-attractive gold and blue tie to send Monica a message. The story is she gave him the tie, saying that when she saw him wearing it on TV she'd know she was close to his heart. So, if he shoved it in his pocket just so she could see the tip of it hanging out, what do you suppose that was supposed to signal? Come to think of it, ties

41

always point downward, so any tie Bill would have worn would have been an adequate signal for "See ya later, and bring those Altoids," don't you think?

So what if it means that the spy codes coming out of the White House are less Tom Clancey than *Teen Beat Romance*? This new form of Dress Code is fun and could lend an atmosphere of winking intrigue to any proceedings, even those not involving a grand jury. Now's your chance to try some tie signals out on that particular someone you can't be direct with, so when they see you on TV they'll know you're thinking of them (okay, we both know the only time you're ever going to be on TV is if the local news comes to Publix to watch people buy water and batteries during that mesmerizing hurricane coverage, but just play along, okay?)

Tie slightly loosened: "Casual date. I'm not Mr. Right, I'm Mr. Right Now." Tie starched stiff as a board "I do not need Viagra, Let's go." Clip-on tie: "My mother picked this out. You remind me of her, lady." Tie tied like a noose: "Wanna see my etchings? They're quite well-hung." Bow-tie: "I've got Viagra." Bow tie pasta in place of actual tie: "The nurse doesn't know I'm gone. I don't have much time." Tiara: "I am a big queen, girl, quit following me." Skinny tie with *squared off* ends or leather tie: "I haven't bought any music since *Rio* came out. Please talk to me." Fish tie: "I am blind and mean people dress me. Send help." Grateful Dead tie: "I'm too stoned to actually have sex, and yet I am totally boring as well. Wanna smoke?"

Bathrobe belt as tie: "I am an alcoholic." Bolo tie: "I can stay on for a good 8 seconds . . ." Tie with velcro ends: "Tie me up, but don't tie me down." Tie with a stain on it: "No thanks, I've already eaten." Tie just like Clinton's: "Go ahead, blow me away, but only if you do your laundry once in awhile."

The sad bottom line is, I'd bet money Bill didn't actually mean anything by wearing that tie. The signals were Monica's idea, not his. We're lucky most men can get their clothes to match without Garranimals tags, much less remember the poetic meaning behind their sartorial choices.

Still, the way we dress says something about us, and in yet another gift to the American people, the Clinton presidency has helped to make them say things very specifically. And anyway, no matter what he wears or what it means, none of this mess is worth getting the country in a knot over.

The ins and outs of confessional TV

This column, about the self-outing of Ellen DeGeneres and about how the outing of other people for being things other than queer could be kinda fun, was originally published April 17, 1997. Since then, and despite the fact that it was pretty good, "Ellen" got booted off the air, so we got to see her get personally upset all over again about something entirely different than being gay. The saddest thing about it is, she seems like the kind of person who would joke about personal issues in public rather than cry over them in the first place. You gotta have some empathy for her, though. A lot of us, looking at the state of much of television, are brought to tears, albeit for very different reasons.

If everyone jumped off a social issue, would you? In the biggest strip-tease in recent TV history, the character played by Ellen DeGeneres is coming out as a lesbian. Leave it to the progressive minds of television to make a big hoo-ha out of something we already know. The real Ellen is right there on the cover of *Time* this week, nice and casual, with a nice and casual headline, "Yep, I'm gay." It doesn't get any more direct than that, yet when the blessed event occurs, people will be glued to the set like it was the moon landing, because life on earth is still more shocking to some than life in outer space.

The excitement is so terrific it makes me want to come out about something, too. Look, I'm out on the porch! Look, I'm out on the town! Look, I'm out in the kitchen! Even when I'm in, I'm out! I'm even out of shampoo!

In fact, to exploit all the hype, I'm going to make a big confessional deal out of everything I do. Holding hands in public with the boyfriend: "I'm not sure when I decided I was straight. It's probably because all the girls in my neighborhood growing up were ugly." At Taco Bell: "I always suspected I was different, but when they finally came out with soft tacos I knew then there were others like me and I felt totally validated." Drunk in a bar after singing, "I'm a Little Teapot": "Got sumpina tell ya. I'm a dork. Really big dork. I thought it would be hard to find other dorks, but lookatcha. Here you are! I don't feel so good. Let's all get a house and live together! Zzzzzzz."

Confessional television is nothing new. In the '60s Liz Montgomery and Barbara Eden alerted us to the prejudice shown toward witches and genies. In the '70s Archie Bunker outed racism and Maude outed sexism with shows that, as *Time* points out, were much too mature to be popular today. Then in the '80s everyone came out as an alcoholic or a drug addict, and later we found out how many people had been sexually abused, in what my sensitive, insightful editor calls "the incest craze." Like it was Pogs. And now Ellen is coming out. Those who think this is a one-trick pony have another thing coming. With this new direction there are tons of things to anticipate in her show. Will she try to become a folk singer? Will she quit her job to coach volleyball? Now that she's a lesbian, will they have to take the "Humor" section out of her bookstore?

In fact, a lot of people on television might benefit by coming out about things we already know. People like: Jerry Falwell. *Time* told DeGeneres that Falwell had called her "Ellen DeGenerate," which the star deftly jumped by saying, "I've been getting that since the fourth grade." If Falwell would come out and say, "I'm a petty, mean-spirited, holier-than-y'all pitchman who knows as much about the afterlife as the Heaven's Gate cult," who knows? He might lose a million viewers but gain a million others who don't think you get to heaven by calling people names.

Martha Stewart. *New Woman* magazine reports that at a benefit luncheon, Miss Perfect replied to one person's lament about feeling inadequate by saying, "That's your own problem. You have to figure it out yourself. I have." Everyone would watch "Martha Stewart Living" if she would confess, "You think I want to sit around making festive centerpieces out of my toenail clippings? I don't want to, I have to. I have excessive-compulsive disorder and am so anal-retentive I can secretly use my heinie as a duck press. I am affiliated with K-mart! Do you think that's glamorous?" and then break down in a torrent of tears, which she would neatly save to use later in soup.

Michael Jackson. If he called a press conference and said, "Look, I'm not going to lie to you. I'm crazy. Nutty as a Snickers. I carved up my face so I look like a wig head. I named my kid Prince. What else do you need? Just watch what I do next." Every one of us would.

For a voice of authority I asked an actual lesbian what she thought of Ellen's coming out party. "I wish the hell they'd all just stay in," she said.

You have to dig for it, but she's got a point. Entertainment was invented to give us a break from reality. With all these confessions on TV, we might find that we desire more facades and create them ourselves. Then everyone could walk around acting dignified, self-confident and pleasant just to get away from all that damned honesty on the tube. I, for one, would appreciate a little more phoniness of this kind from others.

In the meantime, we applaud Ellen, look forward to the show and remind everyone that while she may be dealing with a real issue, she still has a script that will tell her what to say and do and we don't. Ellen may be out, but she's not out on a limb, like the rest of us.

Farrah: still ahead of her time

Just over a year ago, Farrah Fawcett made an appearance on a talk show in a less than composed state, an appearance which became the talk of the other talk shows for the next week. This piece was written in defense of the woman all women hated and desperately wanted to be in the mid–1970s.

It's really OK that I didn't see the Farrah thing on "David Letterman." The inane ravings of a former starlet don't sound like a surprise to me, and besides, I saw Peter Fonda's speech at the Florida Film Festival. One skinny, old celebrity famous for doing a single, unusually sexy project a hundred years ago, talking like their brain had caved in from drug use, is enough for anybody to take in one week.

Because tabloid reporters trail celebrities the way street sweepers trail defecating horses at Disney

World, you didn't have to see Farrah's verbal hemorrhage to know all about it. Overnight she was on so many covers on so many impulse-buy racks, looking boney and cornered, that you got the impression these were true sick-bed ravings, so disturbing that at any moment they were going to take her away in what my mother sensitively refers to as The Cookie Truck.

Poor Farrah. If the tabloids all ran banner headlines every time you or I said something that begged a straight-jacket fitting, the world would be out of paper 10 minutes from now. But to top it all off, there was a seemingly minor post-Letterman incident that happened after she did the "Conan O'Brien" show. Farrah overheard a couple of women sniping about her in the ladies room and had the cojones to confront them. They said they were disappointed in her for making a *Playboy* video after she had triumphed over all that with strong feminist roles like the one she played in "The Burning Bed." Farrah was reduced to tears.

Now I know it was just a second-hand conversation in a backstage toilet, but don't kid yourself. Plenty of important things happen in the bathroom, and this is such a parable that it might as well have been a scene in a movie on the Lifetime channel. It's the pitting of women against women, a divide-and-conquer move through which none of us win. Farrah, after all, has been through enough that she shouldn't be crying in the bathroom over a few catty remarks. She helped to inspire a new word: "jigglevision." She was The Great Equalizer of junior-high girls, ensuring that not just some but all of us would look like Queen Doofus of Dorkoslavia in that haircut we all wore like a CCP uniform. Then, to prove she was a serious actress, she dove into movies like *Extremities* and succeeded. That's a big risk for someone who built a high and narrow career on being beautiful. She even played Raquel Welch's lover in *Myra Breckinridge* way back in 1972, long before the chicest accessory a girl could have was a girlfriend.

Then came the recent *Playboy* video. From the clips we've seen, it documents Farrah doing art. She does this by slathering her naked self with paint and rolling around on canvases that she then hangs in her home. (They are not for sale.) This, more than anything she said on a talk show, might be evidence that she is one beer short of a six-pack or any other cute euphemism you might want to use for crazy. But it isn't exploitative, and it isn't responsible for the degradation of women. It also isn't art, which is the only really bad thing you can say about it. If she had stuck a couple of paint brushes in her cleavage, did a shimmy and came up with *American Gothic*, or even a game of Hangman, that would be art. But beauty is in the eye of the beholder, and Farrah thinks art is her breast prints. You are hereby excused from Art Theory I, since there really isn't any.

You are not, however, excused from Feminism 201, the "2" indicating that we're hoping to graduate upward and away from some of the arguments of traditional feminism that have pitted women against women in the past. The thinking in that bathroom seemed to be that being proud of your body and sexuality is in conflict with women's quest to be taken seriously. But all it does is put a self-imposed limit on our choices, the in-house equivalent of "She's asking for it" and "Who does she think she is?"

Farrah's *Playboy* video is a far cry from skinny models seducing young girls into look obsessions. Her *Playboy* audience is men, whose unabashed desire is something that she's going to make another mint exploiting. Instead of asking "How could she do it?" women ought to be asking themselves how come they could identify with her in victim roles, but not when she's an older, exuberant success making a choice to do something just because she felt like it.

Until women can allow each other to be beautiful, serious, sexual, funny, kind, demanding and smart all at the same time, all those things we like about men, we are going to continue to get pigeonholed—and a divide-and-conquer downfall will be the result. That ain't no way for a lady to treat a lady. Women should finally be comfortable enough in their grown-up clothes to let other women have a little fun.

And sometimes, the most grown-up fun you get to have is with no clothes on at all.

Girls just wanna have—huh?

Assuming you have friends, ask what they've been doing. Ask if it was fun. Some will say "Oiyah," the equivalent of "Oh yeah" as one word, with the "Oh" much higher than the "yeah," meaning it was so great they can't take you there. Usually they answer in a thin, soprano "Yeah?," meaning they're not really sure if it was fun. Sometimes you'll get, "Well, I don't know about *fun*," as if you had asked something really degenerate ("Well, I wouldn't say *hermaphrodite*"). Your court-appointed therapist will tell you that fun is important to your mental health but lots of people think they're too busy and important to have it. Fun can be as easy as redirecting your attitude but often, like rain or passion, fun can't be invoked. The best you can do is give it directions and hope it shows up at the party.

The Fun Book: 102 Ways for Girls to Have Some, by Melina Gerosa, is a new book that supposedly will help fun-starved femmes with suggestions that are really supposed to drop a firecracker down your pants: "Buy a pair of fuzzy white terry cloth slippers." "You shop, he cooks." "Call in sick when you're not." Oh, catch me. The real fun is imagining how this trite waste of trees got printed.

Few other suggestions have enough spark to light your Lucky, either. For example, "Use your meanest ex-boyfriend's T-shirt to clean the bathroom." I don't care if you're using his hair, you're still cleaning the bathroom. For fun that doesn't involve you coming into contact with the toilet, put his picture into the catbox. Every time you hear those paws scratching up a storm in there you'll be less pissed off, he will be pissed on and you'll get a big laugh out of it. Having a puss you can count on is fun.

"Become an expert in something exotic that interests you" is a good idea. Gerosa suggests as topics "pearls, single-malt scotch, orchids," which sound like accessories you'd spot at the Golden Dusk Assisted Living Facility's "Happy Birthday Gert, 94 Years Young!" party, or the next day, at Gert's wake. Still, it's fun to be a know-it-all about something. I, for example, am an armchair primatologist, which allows me to say stuff like, "Did you know a female baboon's genitals swell up and turn bright red when they're pregnant so you can spot them from across the jungle?" Clearing a room is fun. We all know you can have lots of fun in bed (or on a diving board, or in an unoccupied train car, assuming you're a tramp, which could also be fun; I wouldn't know). While stating in her intro that fun doesn't require money, Gerosa suggests, "Splurge on Battenburg lace pillow shams and . . . pure Egyptian cotton sheets." They probably have coupons for those in the Penny-saver. Better still, go to someone's house who has these linens, cut out eye holes in them, put them over your head and come down the stairs going "Oooooh, I'm the ghost of your expensive sheets." Being mean is fun, too.

Personally, I think it would be fun to get a bloated advance from a publisher to scribble down a bunch of nonsense, but since you're the next best thing, I'll try out my alternative suggestions on you:

Wear a tiara and carry roses to have your driver's license photo snapped.

Draw big red lips on the cat.

Take a stick of butter, let it soften until you can reshape it into a square, then freeze it. When company comes, put it in the soap dish.

Flash a bus.

When the mayor walks by, say, "Nice ass!"

Base all your decisions for the week on what the Magic 8 Ball says.

Have sex.

Tell your friend that you're going to give them a really great all-natural facial, then just throw a bunch of junk in the blender (cantaloupe, ravioli, Milky Ways) and slop it on.

Play strip darts.

When a guy is terse with you, say, "God, you're such a bitch, you must be getting your period."

Tell gossip using sock puppets.

Go to the beach.

Fill a piñata with eggs.

Take the mash notes your ex wrote you and send them to his new girlfriend with your name crossed out at the top and hers written in using crayon.

Go to the store and cross out the suggestions listed in *The Fun Book* and put these in using crayon.

Gerosa does include some fine quotes from some fun women, quotes that are better than most of her suggestions, quotes like, "It's the friends you can call up at 4 a.m. that matter" (Marlene Dietrich) and "Be happy. It's just one way of being wise," (Colette). With those kind of friends and that kind of attitude, you don't need a book to help you have a good time, especially this one. It's OK, but I don't know about fun.

Golf curse

Something struck me." From this phrase one might conclude that the speaker was struck by a thought, an idea, an epiphany of some impact. The other day when something struck me with more impact than any idea I've ever had, it was a golf ball.

When you are struck by a golf ball, thoughts, ideas and epiphanies hit you as well. Like the thought that golf and drooling are neck 'n' neck for Most Imbecilic Pastime Ever, the idea that it should be banned, and the epiphany that golf clubs would look better wrapped around the necks of golfers like Easter bows.

You may think this is the hysterical prattle of the victim of a random silver-spoon drive-by. But I'm not the only one. The very day before I got bopped, the Associated Press reported that James Henn, a New York investment banker, was knocked unconscious by bond trader Alan Greco. Henn (a non-golfer) is suing Greco (a swinging bozo) for $3 million. A judge said that Greco's failure to yell "Fore!" and his crappy playing skills could make him liable for the accident.

While we await the verdict, let's look at some hard evidence why the game of golf should be sentenced to extinction.

Golf originated in Scotland, also the birthplace of haggis, the tam-o'-shanter and Sheena Easton. The motives of any people who eat sheep intestines, wear head pom-poms and unleashed the singer of "Sugar Walls" should be considered highly suspect and probably a radical joke.

Smarter Scots, on the other hand, thought golf was stupid. In 1457, James II and the Scottish Parliament tried to get rid of the game because it was dopey and attracted men away from the more useful sport of archery.

Further proof of golf's inanity is found in those who play it. First there's Bob Hope. Bob Hope has to be at least 206 years old. It's an insult to actual athletes to refer to anything that a bicentenarian can do as a "sport." Riding a cart, sipping a Tom Collins and getting up to hit a little ball every few minutes, well, Sunny Von Bulow could do that with a little aid.

Another famous recreational golfer is Dan Quayle. According to Quayle biographer Joe Queenan, the former VP played 45 holes a day as a youth, grew up on the 11th hole of the Paradise Valley Country Club in Scottsdale, Ariz., and told Bob Woodward and David Broder that he would often quit work as presidential understudy at noon to hit the links. What does this tell us about golf? That spending unnaturally long periods out in the sun, emptying your mind to attain the concentration the game is said to require, might cause you to keep your mind that way and lead to PR debacles like "potatoe." What a terrible thing to lose one's mind, or not to have a mind at all.

Of course, the most famous recreational golfer of all time is O.J. Simpson. This is probably where he learned to slice.

Although statistics on golf-related deaths among humans are surprisingly rare, the AP reported in 1994 that "a chemical widely used to keep golf courses lush and healthy is killing fish, birds and otters and might pose a threat to the state's drinking water." The U.S. Department of Agriculture wants voluntary restrictions on the manufacture of Nemacur, a pesticide used to control microscopic worms that particularly plague golf courses. They're studying why it kills wildlife and to what extent it has contaminated groundwater. The chemical was responsible for at least 10 major fish kills in Florida, and at least 40 percent of our golf courses at the time were using it.

Speaking of death, the golf course where I got bopped while walking on a public sidewalk was the Winter Park Country Club course, right across from the cemetery. When I spoke to Steve Lundblad, the course's pro/manager, he said that in his 10 years there, I was the only person who bitched about personally getting hit by a ball. Usually, he said, it's just cars that get hit.

As to why people seem to enjoy this activity, Steve says that for some it's a self-competitive thing— you're always trying to beat your own score. Also, it's something you can do on your own. So doesn't this make it the ideal sport for moody loners?

If that weren't alarming enough, someone really should step in and do something about those clothes. If they can declare junk cars on the lawn an eyesore, they certainly ought to be able to declare tartan sweaters, madras jackets and pants with little whales on them to be an aesthetic hazard.

But as long as we're living in a democracy, we're going to have to put up with horrible taste, including the possession of firearms and nine irons. Some people don't like to see sex on TV, but in a democracy, we're stuck with it. Personally I wouldn't mind if my kid saw sex on TV and grew up one day to have sex. But I'd pass right out if he watched too much golf and grew up to dress like Shakes the Elderly Clown.

Hyllybylly vampyres

Gomer Pyle became the dark lord of a blood-drinking cult of the undead into which he initiated Opie. After driving to Hooterville to pick up Ellie and Jethro, they came back and beat Granny and Uncle Jed to death. Allegedly.

If you had to explain the story of the Hillbilly Vampire murders to anyone unfamiliar with Lake County, Florida, the above translation may be helpful. If you're still in the dark, well, there were some kids who thought they were practicing vampirism in Eustis, drove up to Kentucky, got themselves some more vampires, drove back home and killed the parents of one of their initiates at her behest.

On one hand, it's enough to make any Floridian who has all their teeth and whose house is stationary hang their head in a Jobian way and wonder, why? Why is it that we are the Bermuda Triangle of terra firma? We already have highway shootings, recluse spiders and Jimmy Buffet, and now, oh great, there are vampires out on Highway 19. Isn't that just typical?

On the other hand, if there were a story like this on the front page every day, more people would learn to read. The local daily media—which knows, of course, that anytime you find an empty beer can and some ashes that teenagers have been practicing Satanism—has told the story with prose so purple you'd think they'd been in a fight. (They also noted that the head vampire liked to be called Vesago, and that nobody knew what that meant. Even I know that Vesago was the teenage undead Satanic murderer in the movie *The Hideaway*, and how do I know? Because he was as cute as a bug's ear.) What more can there be to a story that has everything: blood drinking, self-mutilation, adolescent melodrama, weirdo parents, alcoholic parents, dead parents? How about a vampire who worked at McDonald's?

Bite sighs

When the back country vomits up freaks like these, people tend to get scared, like there's a bunch more out there. It's just not true. Let's take a look with the lights on, shall we?

These redneck vampires aren't very bright. For one thing, instead of turning into bats and swooping down on their victims, these vampires piled into a Buick Skylark and hit the road, which is how the police ended up catching them. It must be awful to go through eternal life being dumb as a carp. One of the vampires, as seen on the TV news, appeared to have enough zits to cover the whole class of 1997, substantive evidence of his vampirism, as he could not see himself in the mirror or he would never have left the house.

And that's just the home team. We picture the Kentucky vampires in an even less flattering light: sitting on the porch in black overalls whittling stakes to pound through the hearts of the vampires they're feuding with in the holler over yonder; unable to find any virgins because can't none of the girls outrun their cousins; forgetting whether it's night or day they can't go out in; not being able to bite anybody because their fangs turned black and rotted out of their heads.

See there? Nothing to be afraid of. Our faith was confirmed by Lake County resident Herb Anderson (not related to one of the suspects, also named Anderson), who we asked if there had been a noticeable upswing in Young 'Uns of the Night in his area. "I thought there was," he said, "I thought I saw some of them up at the Handy Way. But it turned out to be some of the Rainbow people. They sneak into town to eat beef jerky. I thought I saw some blood, but it was probably just hot sauce."

Right sighs

Obviously the deaths of Richard and Ruth Wendorf are the worst part of this whole saga. But what really chaps the butts of those a little more distanced from the whole thing is the likelihood that fanatic Christian or conservative types are going to do the "See, toldja so" dance right in the direction of all those poor kids out there with dyed black hair and a dislike for sports and other wholesome activities. Now they're going to be able to point to those harmless Addams Family accessories, goth rock and literature and cite it as the building blocks for murder. Caught red-handed with two corpses, it's not going to be easy for anyone to say, "Oh yeah, what of it?" Because unless you count piddling stuff like, you know, 20 people hanged in Salem, those injured or gunned down in abortion clinic violence, nine Crusades including the Children's Crusades in which thousands of children were starved or sold, Protestant vs. Catholic violence in Ireland— unless you're going to stand there for a few days counting up all those bodies, Christians are beyond reproach.

Really, simply continue to follow the rules of safety you always do—don't travel on strange, lonesome roads at night; never let strangers in; wash your hands when you're done—and you should be fine and virtually vampire free. But it couldn't hurt to go a little heavier on the garlic than usual. Bone appetite.

Criminy, what an endless parade of freakishness this case turned out to be. In the final outcome, lead vampire Rod Ferrell confessed to the murders in an attempt to get the jury to spare his life, something which, if he were really a vampire, shouldn't have been a big problem. But the poor whacked-out, screwed-up, never-stood-a-chance head-case of a kid realized at some point in jail that he actually wasn't an immortal and better give some thought to this whole Laws of Nature thing and now. He got the death penalty anyway. His mother, Sondra Gibson, was allowed to postpone her probation for the sexual corruption of a minor (she tried seducing one into the vampire cult) in Kentucky so she could be closer to her son in a Florida jail as he awaits the death sentence, and I've heard she's working in a McDonald's in Umatilla. It all begs one question: What is it with vampires and McDonald's?

An attraction that's a real mother

You'd think the only virgins in windows were in places like Bangkok and Amsterdam, but it's not true. There's one in Clearwater, off Highway 19 and right across the street from the Kash 'n' Karry. And this is the Big One, the Cherry Royale, the mother of all Virgins, the Virgin Mary.

Her image is strangely imprinted on the windows of the Seminole Finance Co. there, joining the ranks of knotholes that look like Jesus and clouds that resemble Elvis. A Seminole Finance receptionist told us they had seen something there since 1994 but thought it was just damaged glass and were going to have it replaced. Then a customer came in to make a car payment, saw what the image resembled, and called the media. Since then almost half a million people have come to see it.

Since tours, rants and benders are the only things we get to go on, we thought a pilgrimage would be a refreshing change, although we know that pilgrimages are often ridiculous, even perilous. Take, for example, the 113 pilgrims, nude and smeared with ash, who croaked in a snowstorm in the Himalayas in August. They had all trotted off to worship a stalagmite thought to be the phallus of the Hindu god Shiva. The only way the story could have been better would be if the holy wiener had fallen on them.

Knowing that such surprises often greet the pilgrim, we should have not blinked when we began our quest at a gas station and were told the car needed a bit of work. An entire day and $300 later our faith was a bit less spiffy than the car. Pilgrims just have to face this kind of crap. That, and detractors who call and say, "Too bad you didn't get to go today. I heard on the news that (the two-story virgin) walked out of the window and started stomping people."

We did make it to Clearwater and into the parking lot where one young pilgrim was yelling, "Use your eyes!" at some older pilgrims who walked in front of his car. With all the canes, walkers and wheelchairs poking their way to the Image you'd have thought this was Lourdes. Then you'd remember it's Clearwater. There are more canes, walkers and wheelchairs here every day than Lourdes ever saw, and the real miracle is that the dead are up and around, wearing peach and driving.

They were all over the parking lot at Seminole Finance, too, along with the young, the tourists, the folks selling Mary T-shirts for $9.95, plus all the other thousand people an hour now said to be visiting It. And when you cross the parking lot, the It is very distinct: a prismatic picture of a veil and lines that drape just as the fabric would hang on small shoulders with folded hands. As glass defects go, this one is a pip.

The landscaping wall was covered with more flowers than a Rose Bowl parade float and enough candles that, if we melted them down, we could have waxed the legs of every pilgrim there, and even some of their bikini areas, if asked. But most interesting were the notes. One in a sealed envelope just said, "To God," probably a party invitation. Some said, 'Thank you.' Some asked for help with illness or weight loss. Some asked for money. Some were memorials. One simply asked to "make us better people." The question came down to what the question always comes down to: Is this chick really a Virgin? Of course everyone I asked said yes, except for one visitor who said he thought it was just a trick of the light. My own mother, standing right in front of It, said she thought the image "could make a person convert." Later on the road out of town I asked her if she was serious. Did she think it was a miracle? No, she said, "not with all the crap going on in the world."

Holy crap, she's right. If you were the Mother of God and wanted to give people hope, would you end wars? Cure AIDS? Or stick your own hazy image in a Clearwater window, something David Copperfield could do in his spare time?

The road out of town, incidentally, led to Tarpon Springs, where I once pilgrimmed to see an icon of Mary that was said to cry real tears. But while there were plenty of tourists whacking down beers by the sponge docks, no one was beating down the doors to the churches. Even holy images, it seems, are no match for the fickle mistress of fate.

On the other hand, who cares? The image is remarkable. It was fun. And it gets people to shut up and think for a minute, about possibilities, about miracles, things we never have the luxury of thinking about in our thin little lives. It stretches our thinking to include wonder we thought we'd lost. As a cheap magician in a movie once said of illusions, "People need them like they need the air."

Oh, and a little cash wouldn't hurt, either.

We know sex sells; why shouldn't it be sold?

When Hugh Grant took up with that hooker in a car in Hollywood, he won himself more public recognition and me my first award from the Atlanta Chapter of the Society of Professional Journalists. Apparently the panel of judges was just as horny as Hugh was.

In the 1970s they had a lot of great, crappy, made-for-TV movies about hookers and how you should never end up as one. I watched all of them and walked away with the impression that being a hooker was really very glamorous. They were the only people besides movie stars who got to wear flashy, sexy clothes, tons of makeup and flaunt their bodies. And they got paid to have sex. Sex was something everyone wanted; getting paid for it looked like a good deal to me. No notion of morality entered my Catholic school head.

Of course all the johns were going to look like Hugh Grant. Everybody is very curious about The Englishman who Went in a Star and Came Out a

Felon. He lives an ivory tower life with a super model. Why pick up street trash? It's like choosing the bus station bathroom over the one in your own home. What was he thinking?

The answer no fan wants to hear is, "He wasn't thinking of you." When Hugh Grant picked up Divine Brown, told her it was his fantasy to have sex with a black girl and that he couldn't afford the extra $40 for a hotel, he was not thinking about ruining his image, wasn't worrying about throwing away everything you wish you had. The reason the fall of the Hero Next Door is such a big deal is that it upends our notions about what we're supposed to want and what we're supposed to shun.

We'll start with the sex thing because that's how everything starts. Why, eight years into a comfortable, comforting relationship, would someone step out on the face of Estee Lauder? Because sex with love is a wonderful thing, but the kind of sneaky, forbidden, dangerous sex that went on in that car is no less wonderful. It's just different. There is an energy exchange between any two people who have sex whether they have known each other 20 years or 20 minutes. The outrage is that we're afraid to admit it. If sex without love is meaningless, why does it matter so much when we find out someone just got it?

Then there's the success thing. Long before his arrest, Grant said to *Entertainment Weekly* about his friends, "They treat me like I have cancer. Fame is like this terrible thing I bring into the room. They liked me much better when I was an ordinary unemployed actor."

I know, cry me a river, right? Shouldn't all his success be enough to compensate for a few crappy friends? Saying you can't afford a room makes it look as though you wanted to get caught. Maybe he was just tired of talking about the downside of his otherwise enviable situation. Maybe by going out to prove it, he thought his friends would listen. But we're as hypocritical about success as we are about sex: It's all great until someone else is getting it. Then we can't wait for the fall.

Then there's prostitution. The fact that it's illegal is another screeching example of our hypocrisy. Anyone who really believes in a free market would endorse prostitution, a simple exchange of service for a fee, a sale of something you alone are supposed to possess—your body. The immorality of the act is subjective and shouldn't be legislated. Who is really more degraded, Kelsey Grammer rhapsodizing about Egg McMufffins or Divine Brown fulfilling dreams? The notion that sleeping with men for money is degrading is just another way to get women to feel bad about being sexual. The hookers in those TV movies usually ended up dead—not so Richard Gere in *American Gigolo*.

We say it's degrading to whore out our bodies, but we whore out our spirits, our ideals and our minds every day. We are forever doing things we don't have any real feeling for because at the end of the week there is a check coming our way, and every time we suck up, lie, flatter and dance on the job, we should be able to hear the faint, insincere phrase, "Oh, baby, you're the best." We all do it, we just do it sitting upright, wearing expensive clothes, sometimes over lunch.

The Hugh Grant story does say a lot about our condition but not the simple things you would think. It says we love it when nice guys fall, we crave excitement but despise those who take it, we lie to ourselves that fidelity is real, and we don't understand that if your heart is in the right place your genitals will be too. And finally it says that we've all done degrading things for money and called ourselves "hard-working." But that's just a whore of a different color.

The ultimate makeover

Janet Fogler never called to take me up on this offer.

Dear Janet Folger,
I just read in *Newsweek* about how you were inspired by former football player Reggie White, who caused such controversy by stating "homosexuality is a decision, not a race," to let people know they can change their sexual preference. Good call: If anyone would know about the complex DNA research on the nature of sexuality, it would be a football player.

It's wonderful that your group, the Center for Reclaiming America, and 13 other conservative outlets bought full-page ads in newspapers "standing for the truth that homosexuals can change." Disrespectful, Gladys Kravitz-like busy-bodying is exactly what we need to retain a petty, hostile edge at what otherwise might be a time of serenity. I'm sure if Jesus had a choice between helping those icky lepers and bitching about queers he would have done the latter, but they didn't have gay people back then (no decent margarita glasses). He was only half-human, for goodness sake. I'm sure you all are, too. Maybe that's why you've gone this route.

Anyway, enough of this shameless ass-kissing (though I'm sure it doesn't hurt!). Since you know how people can change their sexuality like it was a pair of socks, I am hoping you can turn me into a lesbian.

Being heterosexual hasn't done me a lick of good. In high school all the other kids at *The Rocky Horror Picture Show* were embracing their gaiety and I couldn't get the hang of it and had to settle for just being New Wave. This was hard on my psyche, and my hair, which turned into 30-pound test line after enough fuschia dye. My drivers license picture carried one of those warnings urging the pregnant and weak of heart to turn away. You can imagine what this did to my self-esteem.

It wasn't a bad childhood experience with women that caused my heterosexuality (although my mother did have a voice that, I'm convinced, scared Bigfoot into hiding). It sounds crazy, but I like men. Not all men, but as a group, the way you like grapes even if you get one that's slimy, rotten and won't get a job like the other grapes. I should hate 'em all because I don't understand them, an attitude I'm hoping you'll help me with. But their affability, their confidence, their voices when they speak softly, the promise contained in their big hands with those thick fingers and . . . sorry. You can see my problem. Know how you hide the Twinkies from yourself because if they're available you'll not only eat them all, you'll lick the frosting off the wrapper, too? Their classic shape, springy texture and creamy . . . sorry. Anyway, you can't play

Hide-the-Twinkie forever; these Twinkies are half the population. So I hope to scratch them from the menu and become a dyke.

Pressure point

Being straight is problematic. If you're in a relationship long enough, everyone starts asking when you're going to get married. I buy plastic forks because I can't commit to a set of flatware. I don't need this kind of pressure. Traditional marriage is what causes divorce, a real roach-in-the-punch bowl to you conservative types. Then there's birth control. As a lesbian, you can have all the sex you want without that awkward "Wait a sec . . ." and hoping that the mood, or the condom, isn't broken. Heterosexuality is the major cause of abortion; I would think you would want to strike this at the roots.

Actually, the best thing would be if you make me asexual. With that kind of free time I could probably get rich and contribute to conservative causes, which, as a sexless individual, I might better understand and cotton to. I have heard that being in a straight marriage long enough leads to an asexual lifestyle, but I just don't have that kind of time.

I hear some therapies attempt to change sexuality using shock treatments and drugs; after enough of that, someone could say you were in love with a toaster and you'd agree just so they'd let you go home (and with a new toaster!). You didn't need to show former queers John and Anne Paulk, who are now married and with a son, to convince me that a leopard can change its spots. I used to hate spinach, but now I like it just fine. Even species isn't a barrier to romance; look at the Springer show. Anyway, I already knew sexuality could be rechanneled. I myself have been able to transfer a great deal of affection from one human being onto objects that require AA batteries.

Anyway, I hope you will consider my request and that we can get to work on this lesbo thing very soon. I'm practicing, and though I'm having a hard time listening to the Indigo Girls, I'm sure enough shock treatments and drugs will help. Your ad featured Mrs. Paulk with the caption, "I'm living proof that Truth can set you free." Amen, honey. Truth is, being free to be who we are is a great thing. If you are free to help, I'd appreciate it.

How Kenny Loggins found his inner self ... or got someone else to find it for him

Celebrities will tell you to eat dirt by the handful if they think you'll pay $12.95 for their book *How to Eat Dirt By The Handful.*

People buy celebrity advice, though, mostly in the form of fitness books by people like Oprah Winfrey. Oprah does so want to be helpful. I do love Oprah, but she could lose weight by vowing only to eat three Tic Tacs a day until she had visited every country in the world and got a diamond as big as a cat's head from each one. That's how rich she is. She could hire the original Greek Olympic athletes to come back from the dead and be her personal trainers. You can't take advice from these people.

Celebs want to help on a spiritual level as well. Actress Leigh-Taylor Young is a proponent of Feng Shui, the ancient Chinese art of home decorating. How you have your home arranged, or how you practice Feng Shui, either frees or blocks up chi, or energy. It's largely common sense.

For example, to make a cramped space feel more inviting, put something there that will make it feel livelier. For many of you this could be a mirror. Or if there's an object which makes you feel negative, get rid of it. For many of you this might be a mirror.

And then, if you're moving furniture around a $100,000 condo, how bad could your life be to begin with? Whether Feng Shui works is, like most things, up to the imagination of the individual, and Taylor-Young says as much. In a book called *It Works For Me! Celebrity Stories of Alternative Healing,* she says that instant cures are about as useful as instant fame.

But *It Works For Me!* is a useful book with remarkable curative powers. Not just because we get to hear people like Diane Ladd talking about the wonders of Juicing ("I was no longer allergic to the puppy. That dog ended up living with us until it died eight years later!") and Olympia Dukakis talking about massage ("By the time I got up off the table I felt less defensive"). The remedies are interesting, but none of them blew air up my spiritual skirt until we got to Kenny Loggins.

Of course, you first have to ask, "Is Kenny Loggins a guy I want to emulate?" Yes, he's rich, but he's remembered for "Footloose." But it's not copying Kenny's method of self-actualization that will help you. Since laughter is the best medicine, specifically when it's directed at someone else, here's Kenny's story, which he tells without a trace of humor.

You see, Kenny's spiritual quest begins and ends with his butt. Colon-hydrotherapy is what he calls it, but we all know that's just a fancy pants term for enema. (Actually it's stronger and as Kenny's therapist puts it, uses a small amount of pressure, so it's got a little more pizzazz and it comes with a therapist.)

"I used colonics to help bring emotional clarity and get in touch with me," Kenny says. If you're trying to get in touch with yourself and you find yourself in your bowels, it might take more than a little water to help you, but anyway.

He goes on to describe the position, the procedure, how enema cures the headaches he was getting during a vegetable juice fast and his relationship with his hydrotherapist, Julia, with whom he felt a sense of trust "enough to pull me back to try more colonics."

Maybe I need a mental enema, but I doubt it's trust that gets anyone to lie on a table and let someone else put things in them. And not only that, you better trust your enemologist. After all, you wouldn't want to think she was sticking gladiolas in there and taking Polaroids.

Anyhow, Kenny reports a cleansing sensation (eeeewwww), an overall glow, and "I began to feel on a very deep level." I bet.

"I had lost touch with my feelings, so I had to take the factors out of the way that might be blocking them." What a load of crap. Kenny eventually married his little enema girl, dumping his wife of 15 years.

Maybe it was deeply spiritual or maybe he just took some brochures home to his wife with a hopeful gleam in his eye and she said, "If you make another suggestion like that, it's not a hose I'm going to stick up there."

But it could be a learning, growing, enriching experience for all of us. If we know that Kenny Loggins found his inner being up his ass, who knows what we might find there, if only we would be willing to look.

The book It Works For Me! *was given to me by Heather Mallick, review editor for the* Toronto Sunday Sun, *who thought I might find something entertaining in it. When I replied by sending her the above story she reacted with disgust and asked that I not send her any more bum stuff (bum is Canadian and also British for hiney). She ran it, however, with a caption beneath a photo of one of Kenny's album covers that read "Sony bills enema-obsessed singer Kenny Loggins' album* Return to Pooh Corner *as a beautiful collection of songs for family listening."*

Kenny Loggins II— A hose is a hose

I once wrote about Kenny Loggins' belief in enemas as alternative healing. He called it colon hydrotherapy, but a hose is a hose. He swore it cleared his head, which gives you a good idea where that was at the time.

I'd never have mentioned this again, but for two reasons. The first is that more of you responded with letters and e-mail to Kenny's potty habits than you have to feminism, traffic and Princess Diana. "More columns about Kenny!" you said, as though he might leak something even worse.

The second reason is, he did.

Kenny left his wife when he fell in love with Julia, the hydrotherapist, the hoser. We all know, because Woody Allen confirmed it, that the heart has reasons that reason can't fathom. Now they're so happy they could just . . . well, you know. As long as she has her equipment with her.

Anyway, its not enough that in the annals of celebrity tell-alls Kenny already stands out. Kenny and Julia had to write a book about their romance, *The*

Unimaginable Life: Lessons Learned on the Path of Love, and they put out a CD and a CD-ROM that came with it.

Before you even ask, the CD doesn't have any sound effects. It's full of swelling, overripe New Age music (plus poetry reading) that sounds like it ought to be the soundtrack for *Labyrinth* or some other movie that's full of puppets. But you can't expect a CD by a pair of Care Bears to have a kick-ass beat or be anything but oppressively sincere. If you like aural Prozac, this is the stuff for you. My Mac rejected the CD-ROM. And I don't really have a problem with anything in the book either. Except for the concept and most of the words.

I admit that I didn't read *The Unimaginable Life* cover to cover, but nibbled, like a vegetarian pecking his or her way through an English breakfast. I don't care for love stories, unless they are mine or my friends, related with lots of conspiratorial giggling. This is partly because love stories are rarely told with any color or texture, but always in that pale pink Life-time channel sort of way, scripted and spiritless, with unconditional heterosexual everlasting love put on such a pedestal you'd think that anyone who wasn't brittle with desire for it was an evil loose cannon and an offense to God. It's the exaggeration I can't stand.

And worse, its showing off. You don't see Oprah in diamonds or Jessica Lange trundling her Oscars around with her in a wheelbarrow. It's vulgar to flaunt good fortune to those who don't have. Love is the same way. A little smooch in public is one thing, but egging people with your romance is geeky, self-indulgent and rude. In fact, if gassing on about love were a thing children did, the Oompa Loompa's would have a song about it.

This is the love of Kenny and Julia flayed open like a cow in a stockyard, their letters and journals and, perhaps every single innermost thought had between 1990 and 1996. Its full of phraseology like ". . . my heart was as full as the fullest, fattest moon and I have never felt so grateful to be alive," and "My heart reached up and took off my abandonment glasses." This could inspire jealousy. They are stuffing themselves so freely at the banquet of romantic love while the rest of us are batting around a prickly pear hoping we can get something out of it without getting stuck. Or it could go a whole other way. Get a load of this passage, where Kenny and Julia find their dream house:

"We sat there together silently taking it in, overwhelmed with a sense of homecoming, as if recognizing an old dear friend quietly saying hello and good-bye and we began to cry.

For an instant, Julia and I saw ourselves living in a little home like this, making soup, writing poetry and rocking babies."

Is it just me, or does soup, poetry and babies sound more like a sentence than a dream realized? If you are a Lifetime channel junkie, this book could cure you. Also, did you notice they cried? They are forever crying, healing and having epiphanies like the rest of us have coffee. They say things like "sacred self-ishness," "I counseled Kenny to feel his life . . ." and "How do you know it's really you when you look in the mirror?" Its hard to imagine when they have time to indulge in the odd colon wash, with all this surrendering, discovering and drifting in time going on. We also find out that Julia once had a boyfriend who shot at her. Well when a person says things like "I have felt the voice of nature come to me in the wind," and "She speaks to me of courage," training a weapon on them might be considered self-defense.

As comforting and connective as it can be to read about love's towering frailty, like in *The Great Gatsby*, or its freeing directness, like in Rita Mae Brown, it can also be a great comfort to know that you're not the only one love has made to look like a big drooling simp. Long story short, one day Kenny Loggins went in to get an enema and this is the result. Usually romance turns to crap. What a reversal this is.

Get thee behind me, Martha Stewart

You used to only see Martha Stewart grinning on book and magazine covers around the holiday season. She figured out how to fit a whole turkey into a flaky pastry crust or some damn thing, and a lot of people loved her.

As usual, the rest of us were asleep at the wheel. Before we knew it, it was Martha Martha Martha. By being just a squeeze more anal-retentive than the Stepford wives, Little Miss Perfect built herself an empire. You know how some people impress you by saving their Old Aunt Jemima bottles for a year and then putting homemade Kahlua in them for you at Christmas? Martha makes them all look comatose. She can take an apple core and an old mascara brush and make a Jaguar out of it. Anything you can do she can do better.

In other words, she's just not right. There's something very suspicious about a person who can run her own conglomerate, be friends with Oprah and prepare salmon according to Native American tradition. She's perfect. Too perfect.

Infernal combustion

If you turn your mind back to the simpler, happier time of the Salem witch trials, you'll find that Martha pretty much would fit the job description the town elders were looking for. Think about it. She's so efficient she seems to be two places at once. Either that, or she has familiars, animals that sort of come from hell's office pool to help out Beelzebub's agents. On her TV show, in her magazine and through her guest appearances, she has a way of wooing women into a lifestyle that's so domestic, even a throw rug would feel the need to get a part-time job. Yet Martha makes this servitude seem glamorous.

Now, the devil hath power to assume a pleasing shape. As Damien in *The Omen* trilogy was a handsome politician, so Martha is a sweetly happy homemaker who makes Sue Anne Nivens look like Joan Jett. To top it all off, she even has a nice caboose. And she's blonde.

How better to lure women into her web of evil, of making them feel bad because they have real-work worries and don't have time to embroider their real linen pillow cases with wool spun from their own sheep while whipping up fat-free tuna-mint truffle muffins for 20?

But the tip-off was Martha's calendar. In Martha's magazine, Martha prints Martha's calendar. In the September issue, the calendar (on page six) indicates that sometime before the month even began she knew she was going to power-wash the shutters on the 8th, harvest the peaches for canning on the 10th, and on the 29th she was closing up the pool. I'm lucky if I can brush my teeth and get dressed in the same day; Martha's going to appear on *Today* and build a fence.

Sacrifice to get ahead

No one's life runs that smoothly and leaves that little room for spontaneous crises—unless they are aided by supernatural powers. But then, if you owned your own magazine, would you want your real diary in it? Especially if aided by a legion of demons? Martha's October issue has a calendar, but who can say whether it reveals Martha's real agenda? What with Halloween and all, we were afraid to look. But we've got a good idea what it might say:

Oct. 19: Take down and press-wash screens. Lecture, Brown University. Clean goat's blood off patio tiles.

Oct. 21: Rosemary's Baby shower. Menu: Wine served in skulls of infants; brie.

Oct. 24: Prepare dinner menus from now till the end of time. Dance naked in pale moonlight at Sabbat. Trim bangs.

Oct. 27: Carve pumpkins; build guest house out of seeds. Lecture, Notre Dame. Throw priest out of window.

Oct. 31: Stand-up buffet for 40 to celebrate infinite power of the Lord of Darkness to raise the dead, protect his emissaries and make sure people stay eager to please. Review homeowner's policy.

Maybe I'm just being an alarmist, and maybe it's actually a flattering thing to say, but it seems a little tough to believe that anyone could make a conglomerate out of junk, the ultimate recycling project, without being favored by alternative energies. Now, if I'm right and I'm found dead, drowned in a bowl of gouda ice-cream with sautéed nectarines served in a piece of homemade pottery, you'll know who did it.

Making Mr. Right

I just broke up with someone. Don't cry for me, Argentina. (That is your drag name, Isn't it?). I break up more often than your cell phone and have gotten good at it, so good that we remained friends. Not like when you say you're friends and then you get a real friend to burn the eyes out of his photos with a cigarette. We're real friends and I'm fine. I only bring it up because its soon going to be Valentines Day and I will get more attention because I have just broken up, the same way that the poor only get trotted out on Christmas.

Still, it was with different friends that I was sitting at Wills Pub, and had I not broken up we might have been choosing our porn names (my favorite is still Beaver Cleavage) or drag names (I've finally settled on Fruitopia) or something more fun; when your heart is secured in the overhead, you feel free to wander the aisles. But when you hit turbulence and your emotional baggage breaks free and hits you in the head, well, its on your mind.

So there I was, quoting a friend who wanted to know how the R word (relationships) could be transformed from a hair shirt to a cashmere robe: "Why," she had said, "can't men just be well-dressed and inter-esting?" Fair, I thought, but her list went on: "And intelligent? And charming? And funny? And rich?" I think she had one specification for each martini.

While I was parroting this list of renovations, I heard a voice behind me say, "Give us a break." It was a guy. I thought he was responding to me, though not directly, which would have been interesting (minus one) and funny (minus two). Instead, he seemed surly (minus three) and obtuse (for a grand total of negative four). Maybe I should have given him a break. But I didn't want to. And I didn't have to.

There's a button-popping freedom that comes with a breakup, a window of dreaming just like after a graduation or a job exit or right before the lottery drawing, before someone else's six numbers are called. And the wish-list, like a day off or a surprise kiss, should be explored while it lasts, because inevitably there will come a time for compromise.

You see, men are very much like bras. The really hot looking ones are never very supportive. The durable, practical ones are mostly boring. They're almost never big enough, and they're all pinchy. I go through them quickly, no matter how well I take care of them, and if I find one I really like I seem to end up wanting two. Free-speech feminist or not, you know you could use one, but they're all a bit confining. If you get one so comfortable that you don't even know it's there, well, what's the point? And you always end up hooked. Men are just bras that can drive. That's Victoria's Secret.

But after a breakup, you're not ready for this reality. A breakup is the time when fate throws open the window of opportunity and strokes you with the hot, florid winds of Could Be. For just that moment, you don't have to compromise. You get to Make Mr. Right. You are allowed to elevate your hopes. And why not? You're not getting anything else up.

You piece him together like Martha Stewart setting a table. He's funny but not the village idiot, romantic but not a cling-on, agreeable without being an adaptably dull slab of human tofu, good-looking enough to stare at dreamily every once in a while but not so good looking that he makes you forget where you put your check book.

I know you're thinking, "Yeah, and when you find him, have the pixies come and tell me; I'll be riding my unicorn to the moon," and you're probably right. Male or female, no one is the perfect balance of rigid Oreo and creamy filling.

There is only one man I can think of with balance. He's an incurable romantic, rich but reckless, a little funny looking, but no more so than Gerard Depardieu or Mick Jagger or any other oddball sex objects. His eccentricity is legend, but evenings at home are his forte. Yes, Gomez Addams is the male ideal. And, sadly, fictional. The closest I've ever come to him is a Gomez Addams candy dispenser, but since

I haven't demonstrated any Geppetto-like purity of heart, its doubtful the Blue Fairy would turn him into a real dasher on my hopes alone.

Wise people don't make resolutions only on New Years. They resolve every day to revamp, improve and upgrade. They have mid-life crises once a week out of fear they've somehow "settled." Settling is something done by old, creaky houses and guilty people out of court. So the most romantic thing I can do this Valentine's Day is to have faith that there are big, steel-belted Michelins out there, and not settle for the crappy little spares that come with the car. Give them a break? Give me a break.

Oh, and if that guy in the bar was talking to the TV, forget I said anything.

This column prompted a gracious and satisfied response from none other than John Astin, the one, the only Gomez, from The Addams Family *TV show who was happy that his wild-eyed creation was remembered and beloved. When I realized who the mail was from, I had to be removed from the ceiling with paint scrapers. A note of appreciation from a legend: it doesn't get more right than that.*

Taking the waters at the Spa Deliverance

You might be one of those people who goes on trips and wants to experience the real whatever, like the real Mexico, not just Mexico City. Or you may be smarter than that.

"Real" excursions are the contrivances of rich hippies who feel terribly guilty about not living "real" lives instead of feeling beside themselves with relief and joy. They don't get enough squalor and bad food at home, and in an effort to feel for those who do, decide to get some on vacation. They fail to realize a few things about the "real" whatever:

That the reason they call it "real" is because, like reality, no one could get out of it or they would.

They build places for tourists that aren't real because the real place sucks. Spending your hard-earned bucks on them is disappointing, like doing knock-knock jokes with an infant.

The Run at Juniper Springs is a real place and as such is not fit for a guide book, so you've never heard of it, I hadn't either until visiting my friend Paige in

Lake County, a cluster of small towns north of Orlando.

We were suppose to go to Alexander Springs, a bring-the-kids-it's-clean-and-safe park with an icy, bubbling spring in the center. I was told that if you don't get there before noon it gets too damn hot and crowded. Because we sat around reading the Sunday paper and bickering over its contents, we ended up getting a late start. According to Paige's mother, Big Red, the Springs was out.

It was hot, Africa hot, and so Paige suggested the less-popular Run. When I told Big Red of our intentions, she flatly refused, flicking her cigarette and saying "It's fulla rednecks, just like *Deliverance*."

Deliverance is an important point of reference in dealing with the South. Everyone knows what it means: knuckle-dragging trogs, usually men, who have so little contact with the world that they have no social standards and don't know that they have no social standards and don't know that it's not okay to wear white in October or terrorize strangers.

People have different ideas of *Deliverance*. To Arianna Huffington, Roger Clinton might be "Just like *Deliverance*." To urban you, Lake County might be "Just like *Deliverance*." To Big Red, who lives in Lake County, "Just like *Deliverance*" meant just like *Deliverance*. If she is afraid, there is something to fear.

But I piled into the car like a dutiful guest to see something real. We drove down backroads, all Lake County has, for 20 minutes and then came to The

Run, so named because it is the inlet at the end of the Juniper Springs canoe run. Like a prissy, professional sun worshipper, I'd packed my little Coppertone 2, my lemon juice to hi-light my hair and my *New York Times* bestseller. Little did I know. Very little.

The fact that there was absolutely no beach by this picturesque river—and even if there was you wouldn't feel safe enough at any given moment to get involved in a book—didn't dawn on me until we got into the parking lot and I saw about 20 pickup trucks. Not half-decent workday pickup trucks, ones that looked like they'd been abandoned by the side of the road 30 years ago and had simply rusted into the ground where they sat.

The people looked like trucks. Aside from ours, there were about 32 teeth in the whole park. It was hard to tell if the guys, with beer bellies like toilet bowls, were tan or just dirty. I noticed a guy missing a few incisors, with hair that looked like something that fell out of a vacuum cleaner bag. He looked like Wolfman Jack, Now.

"Poor thing," Paige said. "He's probably 15."

The women and children were scrawny. Not in fighting shape like the loose dogs, pit bulls, rottweilers, mutts, you name it, surrounded by screaming children, activity and revving engines—just the things that make them snap and tear people's faces off. This could go for their owners, too.

I promised myself, while trying to avoid the wasp nest on the path to the shore, that when asked,

"Whaddaya think?" I would say that I thought they were mean and crazy and to please take me away from this American Nile as soon as possible. But before I know it they were out in the water.

The idea is to take a beach chair and plunk it right in the middle of the shallow water and sun yourself while your bottom half soaks in the cold spring like you're a bottle of bubbly in a bucket of ice.

Once in the water the effect was actually pleasant. I commended Paige on her choice of locations. She said, "Yeah, you never sit due south of a redneck with a beer cuz they just pee right in the water."

In a kind of Stockholm Syndrome reaction, I just sat back and enjoyed the scenery.

Most impressive was the girl with the new baby. The thing looked like a fetus in a dress and could have been born in the truck bed on the way up. It didn't even have its eyes opened yet, or perhaps it had opened them earlier, saw its family and decided to shut them again until death in its sweet mercy came to relieve her. Spring water is quite chilly, and this woman scooped the baby through it, a sort of baptism by ice. It was hard to tell if the baby's wrinkled redness was because it was young or in shock.

The real Florida in places like this is serenely pretty, but the people were far more interesting. Like the woman in the bathing suit that turned see-through when she hit the water so that her bush was more prominent than the ones at the side of the river. And probably likewise crawling with something.

People tied their beer coolers to their chairs so they couldn't escape, but let their dogs run loose. Two guys rowing a canoe past us had big crosses on their T-shirts, the horizontal piece of wood saying, "Jesus," and the vertical one, the post, saying "Loves You." When we asked them why they didn't give us that canoe and walk on the water they just gave us that "Some day God's gonna kick your ass" smile and kept rowing.

The Run wasn't a life-altering experience; no one got bitten or peed on. In fact, I got a nice tan.

But let it be a lesson for travelers. The path is beaten for a reason. People arrange travel guides like they arrange their home to entertain visitors. Because if you saw what it was like for real, you wouldn't go. Be a polite guest and enjoy the show. Besides, you're on vacation. If you want real, go to work.

If Poe had written Pooh

Of all the columns in this book, this one, because of its disturbing nature and peculiar voice, needs an explanation. You know how sometimes you just mix words up in your head, to the point where you are looking at a display of scented candles and one of them says "Strawberries and Cream," but when you walk by real fast you could swear you read "Strawberries and Clams"? Or when you pass a roadside diner that you really think had a sign in front of it that said "Biscuits made from snatch"? One day I got the name Edgar Allen Pooh stuck in my head and it just wouldn't go away. So for Halloween I wrote the story of "The Tell-Tale Heart" as though it were told from a Hundred Acre Wood perspective, so here it is, The Tell-Tale Tail.

True! I am nervous . . . all rabbits look nervous. You would, too, if someone might snatch you up and test nail-polish remover over your newly shaven teats. But this nervousness doesn't make me stupid. It makes me smarter. I know what's what.

It wasn't that I hated Tigger. I loved him! He could always cheer a fellow up with his boundless energy and pathetic need for attention. What about the time he helped get the worms out of my hole? They were falling from my ceiling, right into my tea. We are all God's creatures but they are God's repulsive creatures.

"Don't worry Rabbit. Killing woims is what Tiggerth do betht!"

He threw Christopher Robin's firecrackers at the worms. Of course my ceiling collapsed. Being pests who never go home is really what Tiggers do best. He did have good intentions, which pave the road to hell, so that's where I decided to send him.

It was not his idiotic schemes that were his undoing. It was that tail.

Tigger has a tail that is something like a slinky wrapped in an old sweater which is repellent to the touch. I have observed Christopher Robin use it to send little girls screaming from the bushes in games I'm sure would interest the police. Not only that, it makes this stupid sound, "Boing! Boing! Boing!" You can hear that boob coming from a mile away. And you can't hide when he arrives to "help" you.

Piglet stuck in a tree? Here comes Tigger with the firecrackers.

"Boing! Boing! Boing!"

Pooh sick from too much honey? Here comes Tigger to bounce him like a pogo stick, and vomiting honey ain't pretty.

BOING! BOING! BOING!

With all the boinging, retching and explosions there is no peace here. I don't know how the others stand it. I can't think with boinging. I came to hate the tail and decided to rid myself of it forever.

I was never nicer to the cat than the week before I killed him. When his den was bulldozed to build a yogurt stand I let him stay with me. "What a good friend rabbit is," they said. What do they know. They can't even spell hunny.

Tigger remained clueless but every night, for practice, I stuck my head in his room at exactly midnight and shined my flashlight on his tail. Stealth like this isn't easy for a twitchy rabbit, but I did it. Steady hands. Not the mark of a nutcase, right?

On the eighth night I stuck my head in the door, only this time the click of the flashlight woke him. "Who'th there?" he fidgeted and lisped.

That wouldn't have been so bad but then the tail started.

"Boing! Boing! Boing!"

My eyes spun like bloodshot roulette wheels, I felt my heart pound, sure the little creep could smell me. I lunged into the room and slammed the entire bed right down on his head, which only muffled that ridiculous lisping, his head being made of cotton wadding as one suspects so many to be. The tail darted around like a distressed eel. Finally I caught it. I squeezed and I twisted. My only reward was some fuzz and a "Made in Guatemala" tag.

Just when I thought I could stomach it no longer the tail popped off.

BOING!

I delimbed the body and stuffed it into the couch. It gave the seats a lift, although the blasted tail did, in a rigor mortis spurt, spring up and pop me right in the keester.

BOING!

I stuffed the tail into a tiny, unboingable peanut can and returned to bed, certain the future would be blissfully boing-free.

But soon that Pooh and his little lackey Piglet came by in their nightcaps. Why, oh why, does that bear not wear pants? They heard something and came to check for Heffalumps and Woozels. Did I squirm? Betray one hint that I had just stuffed the couch with their intimate? No. I invited them in. Tigger, I said, had gone to the rug shop to visit relatives. Would they like some tea? Some hunny?

Hunny. A mistake, but did I hesitate? Of course not. I sat there while he slobbered down an entire pot, though their gossiping made my ears ring. I sat right on top of Tigger and those two dopes never had a clue.

"Would you like some hunny, Piglet?"

"No, thanks, Rabbit. But I couldn't help noticing, oh I hope it isn't impolite. . . ."

The ringing grew louder. Why could this simp never get to the point?

"What, Piglet?"

"Oh, never mind. I act like I was brought up in a sty . . ."

This pig, I noticed, had a coily tail of his own and could be next to enliven my furniture, since, as he always said, he was a very small animal. Then I realized the ringing wasn't in my ears. It was outside them. It was coming from the peanut can.

"WHAT, Piglet, do you WANT?"

"Could I have some peanuts? I couldn't help noticing them. I do so love peanuts."

They knew. They had been mocking me. They heard the boinging, but knew what it was. They had known all the time and sat there, waiting for me to crack, to drive me mad, listening to the boinging grow louder and louder and louder.

"Animals! Torment me no longer!" I screamed, handing him the peanut can and hiding my face in my hands.

"I admit the deed. Here! Open the can! It is the boinging of his hideous tail!"

This is the origin of the spring-inside-the-peanut-can practical joke which has been annoying happy party guests for decades.

Christopher Robins' mother sewed Tigger together and he was irritating everyone with his awful chipperness because he was too stupid to have post-traumatic stress disorder. Christopher Robin pulled the stitches from Rabbit's mouth one by one.

And he stuffed Tigger's Prozac into Rabbit's stringy maw daily, for he was a very methodical boy. Soon Tigger was quieter, Rabbit less obsessive and Socialized Medicine returned peace to the Hundred Acre Wood.

Possession is nine-tenths of the fun

Editors will always tell you it's a wonderful thing to get hate mail. They will pour over piles of vile, abusive scrawls written by frenzied readers in fits of anger, all heaped on the undeserving shoulders of yours truly, like Daffy Duck finding the buried treasure in the cartoon, "I'm rich! I'm independent!" I hate getting hate mail. I may say enough things to deserve it, but I really don't like getting it at all and can't share in the "It's good for the paper, it generates controversy" perspective, because I take it all too personally and really care whether some goofball who I would never converse with in a million years doesn't like me.

This column generated more hate mail than almost any other, all of it from Catholics, swarms of them, who were determined to believe that I had committed some sacrilege by inquiring into the nature of the communion wafer, something that I, as one who languished in Catholic school for the first eight years of my education, had a perfect right to do.

Anyway, thanks to this column and the photo that went with it, Catholics all over America wrote and called to say how much they thought I suck. I still have a box of Communion wafers sitting in my kitchen, years later, like that ribbon candy old ladies keep that turns into one big piece of candy after the first two years. I never did have the heart to use them for finger food.

The most atrocious murder since Dahmer gave up liver happened a few weeks back. A man decided that he and his two sons were possessed by the devil. So while his younger son and passing drivers watched, he stabbed his 14-year-old, cut off his head and threw it out the car window.

People actually shut up for a few minutes after they hear this story. Then they ask why this lunatic didn't just go see a priest. As if when you think you're possessed, there is a logical next step.

Now you know, and I know, that demonic possession exists, but only in people's heads. *The Exorcist* showed this with a very exciting story and fine makeup, unlike those boring demons that get booked on "Geraldo." And according to *The Exorcist*, if the devil embarrasses you enough, you get to call a priest.

Having to call a priest is rather exciting because it means you have some sort of spiritual emergency on your hands. For people who treat religion like a salad bar—taking in a little of this and a bit of that until they're so weighted down they can get back to real life—this happens all the time. For most people, it doesn't happen enough.

I had the excitement of having to call a priest not long ago when I went into a Christian bookstore and was able to purchase unquestioned and unqualified boxes of Communion Wafers. These are the little wafers that Catholics believe are the body of Christ. These, I thought, might come in handy. What if you were possessed at the zoo? What then? Out there in public with no clerical assistance for miles? If you have the box of Jesus on your hands, you might be able to get out of this pickle on your own.

But, as much fun as it is to brand a sacred cow, it didn't seem OK to me that any nobody could snatch these up from among the priest collars, also for sale. I called a priest from St. Margaret Mary Catholic Church who right away told me that yes, anybody can buy these things, and at Notre Dame he knew of a freshman who walked around wearing a collar, impersonating a priest. He was trying to get kicked out. It worked.

My priest said that the little crackers (which taste like packing peanuts, by the by) are not sacred until after the priest blesses them, when they go through a process called transubstantiation that turns them into Jesus. Before that they're just wheat and flour and water. If you wanted, you could use them as poker chips. (Here's an idea: Mortify your Catholic friends by setting them out with the hors d'oeuvres at a party.)

Hell's belle

The priest said that they have used regular bread for the Eucharist and that it's just a tradition to use the unleavened stuff. Why, then, haven't they made this ceremony much more pleasant by blessing Twinkies or Bagel Bites and handing those out? What a greater commercial success they would be if the host went Hostess.

I didn't have the chutzpa to ask that one. Whether I like it of not, it's been drilled into my head that these are sacred things, and it's nice to have some sacred things in your life, some things that are inviolate, constant in an inconstant world. It's when they become too sacred—when you forget that all is relative—that what was once a life raft can turn into an anchor. That's when you start thinking things like "possessed," and people can be possessed by other things, things they're holding too close and think they can't get rid of. What was once fun becomes an addiction. What was once passion becomes habit. What was once a career becomes servitude.

Actually, these things make demonic possession look easy. To cure that, just get yourself a Super Soaker, fill it with holy water and blast the Satanic squatter in the noodle. Prudence would suggest that if you just mix daily Tang with holy water, it might prevent demonic possession altogether, like birth control pills or regular flossing.

I'm not sure what the preventative is for taking things too seriously, when the sacred cow becomes bull. Maybe it's not so different from what you might say to the demonically possessed. Just look at your possessor, which could be a boss, a partner or a habit, and say, "You know, this is a big world. To hell with you." Who knows. Say it enough and you might end up self-possessed.

Pregnant space

This is one of those moments where, if I could pace up and down in front of you, wearing a white suit, intoning, resonating and gesturing like Atticus Finch, I would do it. Since I can't, you'll just have to regard that as stage direction and try to remember it while I say this:

Discrimination, my friends, is an ugly thing. Like those horrible little window decals of Calvin whizzing, it is all around us, yet, if not for the keen eye, its offense might go unnoticed. While many of us have a perception that some group, be it the white male establishment, the liberal media or them uppity queers, are taking up the whole lawn and preventing us from fully unfurling the picnic blanket of our life, there is one bunch to whom every one of us seems to have, in silent sycophancy, handed over the cultural car keys and gladly taken a backseat. This shifty sisterhood that has spirited themselves into undue exaltation in our collective eyes are the vessels of future life, the fruitfully multiple, the two-for-ones, in simpler terms, the knocked up.

Before they got their amniotic tentacles into everything, pregnant women were quite interesting. It was fun to stare at them. If they talked about their condition it was to say the little snoochie was kicking. To those of us who enjoy kicking people from the outside, kicking them from the inside inspires hushed reverence. And the thought that something alive is going to burst out of you any second like in Aliens, well, as far as attention-getting, it beats a nose ring.

But having this special status is not enough for these women anymore. The "eating, sleeping, working for two," idea has either gone to their heads and made them greedy, or we're thrusting greatness upon them, unsolicited.

What suddenly brought this cabal to my attention was the new proliferation of "Mother-to-be" parking spaces. Several stores, including supermarkets and a new mall in an adjacent city, have special courtesy parking spots, right next to the handicapped spaces, for women who are pregnant. I guess we're supposed to think it's sweet, that the new mommies only have to take itsy bitsy steps to buy their Preparation H. It's actually unfair that those willing to spend a little extra on the good condoms have to park in Egypt. A spokeswoman for the mall told a newscaster that being pregnant is kind of like being handicapped. Well, not really. Conceiving is bound to feel better than losing your leg in a motorcycle accident. No one sits wondering if their prosthesis is going to be a boy or a girl. Women never become quadriplegic in hopes it will help their marriage. So actually, pregnancy is nothing at all like a handicap, except that it becomes a bit harder to get around. So? Where's the Old Bag space, the Wearing Heels for Eight Hours space, the Big Ass space, the War Wound space, the Bad Cramps space? The Manic Depression space? The Migraine-From-Listening-to-Screaming-Kids-in-the-Mall-That-These-Martyrous-Moms-Can't-Control space?

Should you find these spaces proliferating in your area, ladies, go ahead, park there. I have. I was worried when I saw the police, thinking they might just have anticipated such scofflaw abuse of the stork space privilege, but really, what are they going to do? Ask? Just because you're not showing doesn't mean you're not holding. And it's unlikely that the bag boy gets paid enough to ask you to do an EPT right there by the cart corral.

The next day I got a summons for jury duty. That the jury system is a bad joke whose punch line is always "OJ" is another column. Suffice to say, "Nah," was not on the list of optional excuses but "Expectant mother" was. Why? How is sitting in a roomful of strangers for eight hours a strenuous thing these Uberfrau's shouldn't have to suffer? You'd think they'd want to get off their feet for a full day, and, as potential mothers, they need all the practice being judgmental they can get. Why should the rest of us, who remembered our pills, have to do this, when expectant mothers are ideal for the task?

Even the idea of pregnancy is given special treatment. Television ads for in-home tests show, almost without exception, women who are thrilled with positive results. In reality, women that desperate to find out whether they're pregnant are often not women who want to stay that way. The pyramids aren't this slanted. Depo-Provera, a contraceptive, is promoted with ads that show a mother and an adorable infant, a mixed message fiasco. Are we all so p-whipped by motherhood we can't even fathom that *not* breeding is a damn fine and admirable act?

Personally, I blame all this on the Right to Bomb movement, but then, I blame those overgrown fetuses for everything from hang nails to asteroids and in the end, it doesn't really matter who started it. What matters is that pregnancy loses it's miracle status and goes back to being the routine biological event. After all, the cat can do it, too.

This column ran as it is in the Toronto Sun, *with a slightly more localized version in the* Orlando Weekly. *I have never received more and more vicious hate mail than I did on this subject, including threats of violence on my person and my car. All I can conclude from this is that these crazy, hormonal, humorless pregnant women with their mean streaks and bad tempers are exactly the types who should be raising children; it makes it easier for the rest of us to figure out why so many kids turn out so damn strangely.*

Princess Diana

W e'll all remember where we were," Bill said of Princess Diana's death, the way they do with Kennedy and Elvis. A group of us will one day recount that we were drinking beer at the Fairbanks Inn when a security guard gave us the news. April was shocked that someone could die when they looked so good in clothes. Ben made inappropriate puns with Diana's nickname. I remembered hearing earlier that she had a concussion and thinking "Life is so short, I'm going out drinking." One day I, too, will be dead, and I want to be able to say I participated in something, even if it wasn't something very much.

April was right, though. It is hard to accept that anyone so young and appealing could be subject to the same mortality as a plant or an old person. It seems that much sadder that fate should come to get her, especially because she didn't tempt it, like most of us do.

But Diana didn't do things like most of us do. As a Princess she lead too lofty a life to learn anything from, except for that little bit of domestic savvy she displayed when she hit "redial" to find out who Charles was cheating with. Her other triumphs are just not things we can copy. "Marry a real royal, not someone who calls themselves King Dong," is good advice, but there just aren't enough real royals for all of us. "Don't let that Queen push you around," is excellent advice, but Diana stood up to the real Queen, not the kind that use the men's room which are the only kind we know. So it doesn't really count.

Famous finales usually provide us with some insignificant wisdom, like "Don't mix your heroin with your cocaine," and "Don't sign with Death Row records." But while Diana's life may have been surreal, her death brought up things even peasants like us would do well to consider.

Don't be the good one. . . The good ones always die young, the class acts, the talent, the kind. John Lennon is the one who gets shot. Lewis outlives Martin. John and Bobby Kennedy are assassinated, yet Ted Kennedy survives a dark, watery car wreck. If you are interested in living a long time, do not be the best, be sort of second rate, someone that could be done without, someone who is okay, but not really indispensable. If you don't believe me, I'll get the Ouija Board out and we'll ask the dear, sweet long-dead Eva why she passed on but we still have to see Zsa Zsa doing cameos. . . . but don't be that awful, either. Look at how many relatives young William and Harry will be able to look at and think "Why wasn't it you?" Be mediocre enough to ensure a long life, but just fun enough to make people glad you are going to do so.

Don't Get Too Famous. . . This might seem as sage as "Only get five of the lotto numbers right."

Most of us will never have to worry about whether we're getting burned by spotlights, but still, fame is a desired thing and it's worth considering. Be famous enough to where people want to give you things free, but not so famous that your weight gets more coverage than entire wars. . . . but don't be too obscure. Three people died in that car and the driver was always referred to as "the driver." Be noteworthy enough to at least get your name mentioned in your own obituary.

No one's getting out of this alive. This advice was given to me not long before Diana's death and it cuts right to the chase. I'd bet my own tiara that young Diana expected to be a married school teacher until she was old, not a divorced Princess, dead at 37. She proves that nothing is certain and it could end any minute. So what is it that you aren't doing?

It could be something big, like quitting your office job to be a bellydancer, it could be a small thing, like dying your hair, but there's something you have to say that you're choking on, some secret dream that's starving, some arms you ache to be in that remain free of you. The fears of rejection, failure and looking stupid that tend to keep us from these things should be flattened in comparison with the knowledge that we could be flattened, any second. Diana's death is a right royal kick in the perspective and it's close-up on life's brevity should make everyone vow to do one thing on that "I would if I could," list, to read more stories than reports, to go to the beach more often than the dentist, to kiss and be kissed, and, as Kurt Vonnegut said, keep your old love letters, throw away your old bank statements.

If you're looking for a "... but don't go crazy," you're not going to get one. Few, in the end, regret the things they do, but the things they don't. No one on their deathbed, I once heard, thinks "I should have spent more time at the office."

Stalking myself

Poor Bill Clinton. We all thought once the Paula Jones case was over that he could get back on with the business of running the country and that it would be the issue of sexual harassment, written about below, that would be the next big discussion over the next few months. Little did we know that by August he would be on TV talking about getting lip service.

Almost the minute Judge Susan Webber Wright dropped Paula Jones' suit against President Clinton, making it a moot point whether he dropped his pants, the stories of all the president's women vanished from the papers. Like Disney cleaning up after a Main Street parade, you never would have known that the horses were there, much less that they had left anything behind.

It's kind of too bad really, because it was so much fun to reflect upon. You just don't get that with campaign finance reform. Whatever legacy Bill Clinton might leave, it's going to be hard to shake the image of him standing there with his drawers around his ankles, pointing crotchward. Only Bugs Bunny, Ted Kennedy and little children on the beach can run around without wearing any pants and still be considered cute, and if anyone has learned anything from this episode, it is that the rules about sex are the exact same ones you learned from "Sesame Street" about everything else: When you want something, ask nice and don't grab. Period.

The only area of speculation that is now left to us is whether the judge's decision will further muddy the opaque waters of sexual harassment. And it's a bigger, darker, denser area of speculation than Loch Ness. How do you tell average stupid-ass behavior from stupid-ass behavior that you can sue over? After all, if you could sue every office worker in America for behaving like a buffoon, this country would be one big, white-collar holding cell.

Hands up

And then there are the workers most often victimized by sexual harassment for whom the gray areas have long been impossible to separate into black and white, a group more unlikely to tell their stories than any other because their stories are more embarrassing. I speak, of course, of the self-employed. As a self-employed person, I can tell you, it's shocking and abysmal. As my own boss I am forever behaving in a lewd manner that makes it impossible to do my own job. I can't look in a mirror without checking myself out and making cracks. It's hard to carry on a telephone interview with me always looking at my legs. People who work in an office can at least hide from the offending party. Not me. No matter where I go, there I am, lurking around every corner, stalking myself. I even turn up in the bathroom. It's insane! And it isn't as though I can complain to my supervisor. And the jokes I tell myself—my god! I use language that would make a dung beetle go into a dead faint. I don't know where I get off.

Part of the Jones case involved her inability to prove that she had been thwarted in her efforts to advance or receive pay raises as a result of spurning an employer. I don't know that I could prove it in court, but I'm almost certain that I am what's keeping me from moving up the corporate ladder. I just won't put out. The other day I actually put my hand on my knee. I tried to make it sound all, like, accidental, like my hand slipped. Yeah, right. Like I'm supposed to believe me.

I know, just because I don't have pictures or a friend like Linda Tripp to secretly record what a beast I am doesn't mean it didn't happen. I'm afraid in court it would be my word against mine, so of course I would lose. But on the other hand, I feel guilty. If I'm doing it to myself, who knows who else I'm doing it to? Don't I have an obligation to tell my story and thereby protect others from me?

And Paula's pants thing is small potatoes. It only happened to her once, a million years ago. It seems like I'm disrobing in front of myself all the time. I'm certain other employees don't have to put up with this. I'm pretty sure I could get myself nailed for lewd and lascivious behavior, or at least inflicting mental anguish.

Every time I tell myself about my horrendous behavior I act like its no big deal, and you know, I need this job. I have to work with myself. It just seems like a no-win situation.

And then I hear myself gripe about this stuff and I just have to roll my eyes. Sure, I admit I cross the line sometimes. I don't remember complaining at the time. I never missed a deadline, so the whole thing couldn't affect me that much, could it? As for the undressing thing, that had nothing to do with work, and anyway, you name me one free-lancer who doesn't work half-dressed. They all do it. That's why they free-lance, so they don't have to dress up.

OK, it's not that bad. The truth is, I can tell when I'm just being a stupid jerk and when I'm being a dangerous, sinister jerk. But most women aren't afforded such clear insight into the motives of their bosses and co-workers. The only clear thing seems to be if you think you're being treated disrespectfully, pipe up.

Because the longer you wait, the more people seem to doubt you.

So I'm going to do it. I'm going to report myself right now. As soon as I'm out of the room so I can't hear myself tattling into the phone.

Olympic spirits

(Summer, 1996)

Atlanta—We're sitting in a bar in midtown being hovered over by a semi-conscious waiter with smeared eyeliner, a face like Danny Osmond and a body like a parade balloon. He's wearing a bullet vest like Rambo but little else, and he's got shooter tubes where the bullets should be. He looks like he's trying to sell lab samples of hepatitis. You can barely hear him mumble "Want one?" over the competing sounds from the disco and the highlights on TV of the water polo match between the U.S. and Italy.

In our efforts to pursue this moment to sit in an Atlanta bar and say "Water polo? I thought they were playing Marco Polo," we've struggled enough to identify with that tiresome little scrapper who makes it to the Olympics against all odds. You know the one. Every Olympics we are forced to listen to some Horatio Alger story about Dag Hardluckovich, who toiled in the sackcloth fields of Gloomoslavia since birth while training for the Sisyphus Rock Pushing Competition and, lo and behold, made it to the Games. Usually we listen with zombified apathy. But this year we are that little pest who overcame Fate, and by God, we have now reached these Games and can drive through Atlanta and have our host tell us, "That's Grady Hospital. If you have a gunshot wound, it's a good place to go."

While the rest of the journalists rode first class on company-subsidized flights to Atlanta, we sat on the side of I-75 in Gainesville on the day of the Opening Ceremonies with a broken dog bone. This is the belt that holds the engine to the engine block. "You can drive to Atlanta," the mechanic had said, "but your engine will fall out along the way." Hell, we thought, without that thing weighing us down we'd make better time. We were stuck. We were crushed. Fate, as I read that it would, took its cut.

But having won the gold in making a silk purse out of a sow's ear, we got around the situation: Rather than watch the Opening Ceremonies in a bar in Atlanta, as God intended, we watched them at a bar in Gainesville. What a feat of resourcefulness. How did we do?

You might think you saw the Opening Ceremonies, but unless you were watching this Song of the South with Southerners, you missed out.

The announcer spoke of the South, "its beauty, poetry, rebirth."

"And lots of racist jokes!" came an answer from the bar.

The first thing that got major attention was the pageant of pickup trucks circling the stadium floor.

"They ought to run their dogs in front of those trucks," someone said, hoping for a configuration of drooling, snarling pit bulls to circle Gladys Knight during her rendition of "Georgia on my Mind." Lots of reporters noted the trucks but none pointed out, as the person next to me did, "They have their hunting lights on. People think this redneck thing is real cute but they don't know those lights on those trucks are for shining on an animal so you can paralyze them and blow their brains out." How y'all doin'?

When the dancers in the enormous pointy white robes and head dresses came on, everyone nursing a beer in that single-file line of drinkers thought the same thing but only one, a guy they called Pugsley, said it: "A field of people in Georgia wearing sheets. This is where it changes into a Klan meeting and they lynch everyone from out of town."

Trying to turn the sound down, the bartender accidentally changed the channel and landed on an Itzhak Perlman concert. And someone said, I kid you not, "Look Mama, he can make that fiddle squeal like a pig."

Such a far cry from sophisticated Atlanta. Here a club bouncer tries to lure us in with Olympic mud wrestling, then recants. To compensate, he offers, "They ought to have dwarf tossing. My Daddy took me to see that one time. They really throw them little bastards. Cost ya $20 a pop."

So you can see it was an absolute necessity for everyone to plan a decade in advance to airlift their journalists in to experience this first hand. Fortunately people like me, from smaller places with less ambition, are easily impressed. Here in Atlanta I'm impressed by the NationsBank Building all lit up special and looking like a spun-sugar dessert. I think Coca-Cola ads are art, and don't think it's at all tacky that every available space on every street corner that hasn't been taken up by a T-shirt concession has been filled in by a carnival ride. I hear there are some sporting events going on in town, too. Which should make it all the more exciting. We'll be watching them in the bars just like you, so it's kind of like we'll be watching them together. Only you'll have to pretend that across the street, a guy in the red pickup is playing country music so loud you can hear that fiddle squeal like a pig.

Dirt bags

Standing right in the middle of the overpass high above eight lanes of Atlanta traffic in the most unforgiving heat imaginable is a woman in a hoop skirt and a pair of Foster Grants the color of milky tea. The hoop skirt dress is, of course, peach colored. (Drawings of peaches dot the landscape like stars in the night sky. And it is not my one track mind—they *do* look like little tushes. There is even an Olympic T-shirt that says "No pain, no peaches," possibly coined by some confused person in a hospital bed.) She is flanked by two men in Rhett Butler drag with slimy, greased hair and smiles that suggest their lips have spot-welded to their teeth from the heat.

"Welcome to Atlanta!" they leer at us, and then the Giant Peach in the sunglasses drawls, "Would you like to take some red Georgia clay home to show your friends as a souvenir of your trip to Atlanta?" She speaks in the most contrived accent since Keanu Reeves tried to talk British. She then displays a baggie the size of a wedding invitation filled with the indigenous soil, which is indeed an orange red, the color of good, hot Buffalo wings. It has a calligraphied label that says Georgia Red Clay and when we reach out for it she says, "Five dollars." Our hands snapped back like she had turned into a cottonmouth.

We laughed directly in her poised Southern face.

"You want us to give you five dollars for a baggie full of dirt?

"For five dollars what else are you going to do?"

"We're out here greeting you," they said.

"Can we take your picture?" She said yes, we could, for five dollars. We snapped the photo and walked away, wishing sincerely that she would just try to tackle us in that dress and collect her fiver.

Atlanta spent untold amounts of money on security during the games to counteract terrorism, but fans are being terrorized left and right by marketeers like these, and moreover by the heat. Proving the old stereotype that sports people have skulls approximately as thick as their thigh muscles, the members of the International Olympic Committee believed the Atlanta hucksters when they told them that the temperature here in July averaged in the mid-70s. If anyone from Atlanta ever tries to sell you on anything, remember that this is a town where they actually will try to sell you a baggie full of dirt for five bucks. No wonder someone once burned this place to the ground.

Babies are lolling out of their carriages, face down, drooly, hysterical with sweat and rashes. At the Olympic Village we can admire the variety of faces going by from all over the world—all soggy with perspiration and looking miserable. The wait for the street lights to change is longer than the run of *Cats!*, and as we stand there someone says, "Take a good look at this corner kids. This is where you're going to die." One of the merchandisers is selling these very realistic bird kites that perch way up on the end of pointed sticks and some teenager, eyes skyward and gait wavering from the heat, nearly stabs me in the heart with his dove of peace.

Being threatened by the international peace dove is really not all that ironic of an event in Atlanta right now. On one hand, the Games do encourage a kind of great "The World is Our Clique" community spirit that CK1 and Bennetton have worked to achieve more tirelessly than the UN. On the other hand all this in proximity will bring to the surface like a suffocating diver any due or undue prejudice you have for anyone from anywhere, and magnify it under a lens as thick as, appropriately, the bottom of a Coke bottle. Thank God we're ivory tower Americans who didn't even realize some of the participating countries existed. It cuts down on the number of people we can randomly narrow our eyes at. Andorra? Who ever heard of Andorra? We thought Andorra was Samantha's mom on "Bewitched."

We may be interested in these "new" countries but tend to reserve our critiques for the Vanilla, Chocolate and Strawberry ones, the places we're familiar with, the things we know not to like. Unfortunately the games are beginning again and there is no time to dwell on these irritations. We'll think about that all, tomorrow. After all tomorrow is another day.

Game face

On the walls of the bathroom in the Little Five Points Pub the graffiti reads, "George Bush is a slave trader American Caligula." That's what I love about Little Five Points. There is every possibility that they don't know there is a new president. They may be too stoned, self-absorbed or happy to care.

We escaped to Little Five Points an hour ago. Tunneling out of Shawshank with a baby spoon would be peanuts compared to getting through downtown Atlanta traffic. You know how, if you put your finger down in front of an ant, it will bump into the finger and detour itself into circles if you continue to stymie it in this way? This is what it feels like to drive in this city now, with major access roads randomly closed. It's as though the goal of the city organizers were to leave visitors lost, crying and out of gas.

When I (driving) was told my temples were visibly throbbing and I looked "like an 'X-Files' monster," we deserted the plan to go look at the middleweight judo exhibition (it was going to take place in my car at that point anyway) and went to Little Five Points.

Not to be confused with regular Five Points, L5P is a wiggy pothead piercing tribal dark beer vintage clothes kind of place and since arriving in Atlanta we haven't breathed so freely as when we stepped out of the car here. You wouldn't know the Olympics were going on. There is room to move. Babies are happy. They aren't passed out.

The bartender at Little Five Points Pub is quiet as we sip our mid-afternoon Newcastles in the silence that follows a near-death experience. Then he gives us, in little cups like those for taking medicine, shots of Jaegermeister that are so cold there are ice chips in them.

"Why," I ask, "did we win something?"

"Nope," he says. "That's just the way we are around here." He could mean Atlanta in general, whose people are so genial that this is the only town on the whole face of the planet that could endure this craziness without sneaking anti-psychotic drugs into the water supply. The only sports remark he makes is, "I'm in training to be a gutter punk. If I don't shower for a week and don't change my clothes it will work. And by then I'll be waterproof."

Around the corner is a store called Throb. It has just one Olympic item, a purse made out of an Atlanta 96 license plate. Here, in addition to the regular gear, is a most sumptuous collection of slutwear, vinyl, leather, rubber, feathers, all with prices so inflated they could pop and send underwear shrapnel flying everywhere. There is a girl on the phone with her dad, saying she will too buy that corset, she doesn't care if she can't breathe in it, it's her money and she'll do what she goddamn wants. (I can no more imagine discussing bondage wear with my parents than I could having to call a place called "Throb" to find my daughter.) My favorite sale item is a line of makeup they call "Urban Decay." Instead of names like champagne and tea rose, the colors are "Plague" (dark purple), "Frostbite" (dark blue) and "Mildew" (green).

A few doors down is the Yacht Club. Outside hangs a plastic thermometer reading exactly 100 degrees. "Oh, that doesn't count," says a man across the table who must have been a knock 'em dead looker at age 20. "It's in the direct sun."

"So were we," we tell him. The lady with him has one of those laughs that fills a room like furniture and makes everyone around her laugh, too. She says the ugly shirt she's wearing, which we have seen all over the city, is especially for volunteers like her and some guy already offered to trade her for it.

"What did he ask you to trade for?"

"Just a white polo shirt," she said, and . . . a hundred dollars.

Nothing has ever gotten off my back as fast as would any shirt that someone offered me a hundred dollars for, especially not this designed-by-a-blind-person menage of blues, greens and rings. The weeds and broken glass that festoon Atlanta have nothing on this shirt as eyesores. But she was proud of her work and wouldn't part with this symbol of it. She said she had the weight of her company on her shoulders. It seemed to be the first time she realized it. "My God. I better have another beer," she said.

Then her companions started a game of one-up-manship.

"I saw people having sex right there on that roof the other night."

"Well, Jim's got pictures of a half-dozen people having sex up there."

"Hell, I see people having sex up on that roof all the time."

Both the participants and the voyeurs should get medals in the category of Completely Ignoring the Games in Pursuit of Something Fun.

That's how we ended up at Little Five Points to begin with.

High times

By the fourth day in Atlanta a routine has been established:

A) make attempt to do something Olympic-like.
B) Get fed up.

C) Start craving cold beer with the laughable mania of the bad example in an antidrug/liquor film. Actually the liquor craving has been coming earlier and earlier in the day and will soon start kicking in the night before. And it's not just me. In one of the beer tents near a public transit station, a guy is running around with those little pill-cup samples of frozen drinks. The people he approaches all look at him with a water-headed smile like he is the cutest boy in the class and he just said "Hi" to them, they are so grateful for free liquor.

Deeper inside the tent there are a bunch of listless people drinking beer and watching rowing on TV. God knows where they all came from or how far they traveled to sit in a tent and drink beer and watch television. And rowing, no less. Sure, their muscled bodies are something to see, but how long can you watch them row? How interesting is it? It doesn't seem any different to me than if you had six leaks in the roof and watched to see which one could fill a pot of water first.

But this is just how non-sports-oriented we are. We can't imagine why, in the great scheme of things, anybody much cares who can outrow who, although we are interested in how the Greco-Roman wrestlers can do their time in the ring without getting visibly aroused, because it's the games people really play that are much more interesting to us. Our host Blaine, for example, can endlessly reel off the details of our mutual friend's personal lives whether they really happened or not and it's fascinating. But when watching a

133

news clip of Muhammad Ali lighting the torch, he said, earnestly, "Look at him shaking. Is he nervous or something?"

But we've been trying and will continue to try as long as we can to be good sports even if we don't see good sports, to indulge the like-we-care commentary about every single athlete's Little Match Girl past, to pay $2.50 for tiny bottles of water and to generally try to fit in with what the whole world seems to be fascinated with . . . or perhaps just what the corporate sponsors are fascinated with and will browbeat you with until you feel you have to be interested yourself. We are good sports. We even tried to learn to high-five. After our first big brown beer of the day (it was happy hour in the home country of one of our little international friends, we think her name was Hamma Lamma Ding Dong) we decided it was high time we learned to high-five because we saw a woman in a bar the other night who looked just like Tommy Boy and high-fived everyone and was the life of the party. We put our hands over our respective heads, tried to bring them together and smacked each other in the face and practically off our bar stools. Dammit, before this whole thing is over, we're going to bring home the black and blue for the USA.

The content of their character

It isn't easy living in Orlando and having a violent, almost allergic reaction to "characters." It's like living in Hawaii and hating the ocean. People here think that if you're running anything from a theme park to a seminary, someone ought to walk around advertising it by wearing an oversized fun-fur head sporting a look of friendly idiocy. Every time I see Them, I about-face like Pac-Man. But since there is no self-help book titled *I'm OK, You're Chuck E. Cheese*, I've had to try to figure out my phobia myself.

The answer has to do with control. Even though you don't know who's inside that suit, you're supposed to interact familiarly, "just play along," a phrase people always hear right before they get screwed out of something. But the unseen always has the advantage. Look at God. You can't. Advantage: God.

Or it could be that shaking hands with a puppet feels stupid. You'd think the Miami Book Fair, the most cerebrally stimulating thing that Florida has to offer besides electrodes, would be too sophisticated for these roving carpets. When you're among the likes of Douglas Adams, Anne Rice and George Plimpton, you do not expect big fun-fur paws padding around the same ground. But we were strolling through this very event, seeing these very people, when we saw Them: two bobbly headed characters, a dog and one confused wad that I didn't recognize, all directly in our path. There was no way to dodge them. We were going in.

In midscreed about how much I hate those evil things, I stopped. The wad suddenly looked familiar—the peculiar head, the sparse, artistic face, I am told that my eyes got as big as tires.

"Stinky Cheese Man!"

Stinky Cheese Man, for those of you who have never been anywhere or done anything, is the hero of a children's book. He has a wheel of cheese for a head, green olives for eyes, and two strips of bacon for a mouth. I ran down the half a block to where the ill-shaped creature was standing, looking like a child who had been left alone on the corner wearing the world's worst Halloween costume. I loved Stinky Cheese Man ever since I first saw him at the tender age of 27, with the same sappy warmth most people have for Mickey Mouse or Bambi. If Disney World was Stinky Cheese World, I'd be one of those blithering nerds who want to get married there.

"Are you Stinky Cheese Man?"

He nodded his wheel. "I'm not really stinky," he said.

I asked for a picture. He offered a little hand shrouded in a dirty fun-fur sock.

"Here. You can hold my nub," he said. I grinned like it was a wedding photo. I'm surprised I didn't start crying. People began to gather and I talked adoringly to Stinky Cheese Man as if I had Tom Cruise and Rosie O'Donnell backed into a corner. He nodded his wheel sympathetically. That's when I had another realization: I was looking into his olives.

"I think I have to go now," I said.

While it is a sign of respect to look a person in the eye while conversing, I'm sure it's a sign of many other things, according to your Psych I textbook, if you look them in the olives. I had looked into them to convey my sincerity. I had wanted someone made of cheese to understand that I meant business. But he was looking back at me through the bacon. I felt like people must feel when they wake up with a wallet in their mouth and a crowd standing over them.

The cheese stood alone for a good 10 minutes before someone led him to the children's books area, where he was swarmed by kids. And during the drive home my excitement over my celebrity encounter commingled with fits of brooding. I hate characters. It's fundamental to my sense of self. I enumerated instances—a fire dog at the fair, Goofy at Disney—in which I had avoided them as if they carried typhoid. How then to explain my swooning reaction, over which I puzzled like it was a Rubik's cube? It was as if the guys who used to make the Folger's Coffee switch had done something similar with my DNA.

"What if it were Ren and Stimpy?" someone asked. "Or Cartman from 'South Park'?" The warm cheese glow returned. I would gladly play along to a strange, rude, irregular fuzzball to whom I could fully relate.

Finally the truth hit home, offering solace not just to me but to all who get the creeps when confronted by the characters we have to face. Cheesiness is not always bad. You just have to find the kind that is stinky enough for you.

Naked aggression

(Continued observations from the 96 Summer Olympics)

Everyone brings a little light reading with them on a trip. Blaine, our host in Atlanta, likes philosophy; I like travel essays. My friend Paige has a brand new copy of *Urge* magazine. Hers are the only shoulders that ever get read over.

Urge had sort of an Olympics issue of its own, showing male anatomy from all over the world. It was a pleasant diversion from all the family-style entertainment we had to put up with during the Olympics and which toward the end of our stay we had had just about enough of. But the Games make you get used to seeing beautiful bodies performing amazing feats live, and pictures just don't cut it anymore. We decided to see if we could find some more grown up exhibitions of the human body.

When you find yourself seeking out a strip bar in Decatur, Ga., it's probably time for a counselor, or perhaps a court-appointed therapist, to quiz your priorities. We saw lots of cars in the parking lot of Guys and Dolls, but the crowd watching the girl in red vinyl boots dancing to New Wave was tiny. This, we thought, can't be it. Did business worsen because of the Games?

"Oh, yes," the bouncer told us, "People come (to Atlanta) with their families. And most people who are here to see the games are tired after walking around in all that heat all day. They don't wanna come out to a titty bar." Touché. But what of the packed parking lot?

"That's for the other side," a barmaid told us, jerking her thumb over her shoulder. "The men's side."

How it had not occurred to us, we'll never know. We thought the guys were in the chairs and the dolls were on the stage. We didn't realize there were guys on the stage, too.

Men's strip shows, I think, are like window shopping or watching The Travel Channel. You're not going there or getting that. Why tease yourself? Isn't life frustrating enough? Also, I don't think it's any big thrill to have to pay gay boys with parade-balloon bodies a dollar to smile at me. But we were there to see athletic physiques. And what an eyeful we got. The boy's show was packed, with guys and dolls of every conceivable kind in the audience, with one thing in common: a taste for men.

There weren't any tables so we sat down at the bar. Almost the moment my fanny hit the chair, the sleaze stack dancing in front of me grabbed my beer out of my hand and gave me that sexy look—heavy eyes, open mouth—and made like he was going to pour my beer on his nearly naked body. I couldn't look back—I had to turn away to laugh. "You have to look," he said. "The first one that looks gets to lick it off." I told him the old man across the room wearing the choker had dibs, as he had been staring since 1947. The dancer didn't talk to me any more.

We were told by two girls that it was amateur night. If you think there cannot be degrees of professionalism in bouncing around naked on a bar, you're wrong. It's embarrassing enough if you do it well; do it badly, and you're but an eyesore. As we decreed this, I noticed one of the dancers in the audience was bucknaked. (Not that he was so great but in a room full of clothed people, one naked one will catch your eye.) "I thought it was illegal for them to take everything off," one of our party said. Well, either we were in the middle of criminal activity or nekkid dancing is legal in Decatur, because pretty soon it seemed like every man in the bar was doing it.

Oh, they started out innocent enough. They had their cute little outfits on, their cowboy get-ups, their New Wave drag. Our favorite was the gangsta who wore one of those trendy Mad Hatter hats and threatened everyone with a very realistic looking handgun. Let's just say that when he hung his hat, it was a very well-hung hat.

We estimated we saw 16 live penises that evening, a record in all of our books for one night. And it was kind of fun to be able to stare, though I couldn't for long. I kept bursting out laughing, which is one of the worst things you can do to a penis without touching it.

I couldn't help it. People who think these places should be shut down should see for themselves—they are very unsexy. In fact, they're comical. The men gyrate around to house music with their private parts bouncing around like Flubber, so it's about as erotic as when the unfixed neighborhood dog bathes himself in public. For the icing on the cake, wait till one of them has bent over to talk to the table next to you, which means you get the most up-close full moon you ever saw. For the roses on the icing on the cake, wait till he scratches his ass, which is as close to your face as only your beer bottle should be.

Many of these guys did have bodies of Olympian proportion and we hope to see them in the competition that will be added in the next Games. I don't think you'll ever see a spectacle more aptly termed "ballroom dancing."

Swallow the leader

In sitting down to write about the scandals coming out of the Best Little White House in Washington, I keep hearing a voice inside my head saying, "If everyone else jumped off a cliff, would you?" (What else the voices say is none of your business. They don't like you, though, I'll tell you that). Well, yes, I would. If everyone else jumped over a cliff, who would make the cappuccino? Replace my alternator? Make "The Simpsons"? Clean up that big stinkin' mess under the cliff?

So, I'm following everyone over the cliff, albeit a little late (cushier fall that way), and write about Bill Clinton. Despite the posturing about whether Clinton lied under oath, the sex is the only thing anyone ever cares about, so that's all we'll discuss. But it's not just sex. It's sex with Bill Clinton. Nobody cared about George Bush's alleged affair because he was a creepy adenoidal coot with a wife who looked like she placed third in the Boswell-Johnson look alike contest. Who would want to hear about that saggy, papery flesh pressing up against anything? If they were going to make a movie about Bush, they'd have to shave a ferret and make it wear some little glasses. And the entire nation plugs their ears and screams "Mary Had a Little Lamb" when they hear about Bob Dole's Viagra prescription. Clinton is powerful, sexy and charismatic. Cripes, John Travolta is made up to look and sound like Clinton in *Primary Colors* and there isn't a more sexy, not-much-older man than that.

And we're not just talking about Bill Clinton. There's also Monica Lewinsky. She, too, is sexy. The reason Paula Jones didn't cause broadcastus interuptus is because, let's face it, she's ugly enough to scare a buzzard off a carcass. She got a makeover, but they made the mistake of leaving her head on. Monica Lewinsky may be pretty in an Arkansas Junior League, Gayfers Teen Board, Miss Dogpatch kinda way, but she's still a head-turner so her story is a page-turner. Personally, I'd rather have a president who was having good sex with whatever was handy than one who was unsatisfied or going without altogether. Put it this way: If you had an exam being graded, would you want that teacher to be fasting, on Slim Fast, or dripping melted Dove Bar on your blue book? Duh. People who have their physical needs met are calmer. Better to have a cooler head making serious decisions than a corked-up hair trigger who just might snap and strangle some chump-change ambassador and launch us into a war with Andorra or someplace. I have heard sex described as a misdemeanor, because da more you miss, da meaner you get. Why do you think everyone is so scared of nuns?

Infidelity isn't the problem. All infidelity is just a symptom. The problem is marriage. Plato knew that married people are prone to nepotism and that only a single person, with no interest but the state, could run the state effectively. We, however, seem to demand a spouse from our public officials even though, as Elvis sang, some people just are "not the marrying kind"; requiring them to get hitched is like confining Julia Child to an E-Z Bake Oven. Why, when their range is so much greater?

Besides, while sex partners come and go, and may be as interchangeable as Legos, a good ally is forever. The Clintons have endured more sieges in six years than most couples do in six lifetimes, and their come-hell-or-Whitewater loyalty to each other is exemplary.

Kenneth Starr, eventual historical footnote, has turned up nothing on the most-watched man in the world after spending six years and $30 million of our resources. Give me that kind of carte blanche and I could find hard dirt on the Virgin Mary.

But immunity from persecution isn't in Clinton's contract, so he continues to run the country, propped up by a public that, in poll after poll, seems to think of this as an issue that belongs solely between the

Clintons, and sees the press reacting like a bunch of bored, gossiping housewives, turning the matter into a game of "Telephone" with larger implications. At least that's my view. And it looks pretty clear, even from the bottom of the cliff.

I ate, I drank, I got sick—it was bliss.

Cruising. Depending on your outlook, the word means lots of different things. It could mean driving up and down the same strip, pestering people on the sidewalks and being a public nuisance. It could mean something you do at a bar, standing there with your head going back and forth like a lighthouse, prospecting for flesh. It used to only mean a long, restful ocean voyage for the people who had a sea of money.

Not anymore. Some 2,974,703 people sailed to or from the Port of Miami in fiscal '95. To hell with the former American idea of a vacation, which was to pile all the kids in a hot station wagon and drive across the country, stopping sparingly for food and restrooms and nobody talking to each other by the time the whole thing was over. Today, the ideal vacation is to get on a big boat that's all about having your needs met. Families barely have to see each other on vacation anymore.

It's an attraction I'd managed to miss, thanks to a

recurring nightmare I had in which Kathie Lee Gifford got up and sang and danced about cruises regularly on national television. I've always thought of cruise ships as little more than piñatas for sharks.

Another dubious thing about cruises is their marketing lingo. Get a load of this passage from *Under Crown and Anchor,* a commemorative book celebrating the 25th anniversary of Royal Caribbean Cruise Line: "All on board surrender to an intoxicating indolence, detached from worry the moment our vessel undocks ... the same benign spell is cast on every shipboard conscience."

So are we going sailing or Into the Light? The only time others take care of your every need without you having to so much as blink is when you're in the hospital hooked up to a morphine bag. The only people I've seen who were genuinely detached from worry were drooling in the day room in *Cuckoo's Nest.* Passive dribbling is involved no matter how you look at it. And between that and possible shark encounters, it wasn't something I was going to try.

As luck would have it, I was offered a travel-writing assignment—a cruise in the Mediterranean—which makes me think y'all ought to come over and rub me for luck, because it's not every day something like this happens to a person.

Not long after boarding a vessel that is much larger than any of the buildings where I live, the first thing they did to detach us from worry was make sporadic announcements that if the ship hits a mountain your life vest is in the closet. Then you are supposed to report to your muster station. A muster station is where you go to get a good seat on the lifeboat when the ship hits a mountain. I think it's called a muster station cuz you must get to it 'er you'll croak.

At the muster station a smarmy looking kid in wraparound mirrored shades demonstrated proper use of the life vest and a chirpy girl took roll call. Her perkiness was so Disneyesque it made me feel right at home, although when you enter the gates at that theme park you'll never hear, "Okay, here's your map, the parade's at 6 and here's a cyanide capsule in case the park hits an iceberg."

People with camcorders were actually filming the muster demo. You had to feel sorry for them. They obviously thought this was something they'd want to remember dreamily over a cup of General Foods International Coffee.

After this I supposed everyone needed a drink because this was where the real cruise action started. They were handing out champagne on this boat like a winery having a fire sale. It was good champagne, too, and drinking it instead of watching it get wasted on that crybaby Kathie Lee, you begin to get the idea. Equipped with enough amusements to satisfy a czar— disco, casino, pools, spa, etc., not to mention a gourmet menu, well, one picks up the rhythm of this good-time orgy. You begin to feel that if you're not acting like a pig you've let everybody down.

Never one to back off when the fun gauntlet has been thrown down, I did exactly what was expected of me. At dinner, conversation turned to pleasant subjects like the fact that people do occasionally die on board. It's not the ship's fault, but usually some shortcoming on the passenger's part like old age or a bum heart. They also have a brig for unruly drunks or thieving waiters. So it's a lot like home, only without cabs.

Speaking of transportation, it's also very easy to forget on a cruise that you're actually going somewhere. It's like one of those office parties where there is actually a point to getting everyone together, like Christmas or an award, only by the time the main event gets off the ground the crowd is so boozy they are far more interested in getting the hosts' dog high. You get so involved in your own little world that you forget you've gone halfway around the real one. I've been in pleasure-woven stupors that have caused me to miss Christmas, but never thought I would come within a hair's breadth of missing France.

Now it has often happened on dry land that I've awoken in such a state of fun-related illness that, after checking to see I'm not wearing a toe tag, I have vomited forth whole pieces of my childhood memory. This familiar feeling occurred the minute my eyes opened one morning on this voyage, only this time it wasn't my folly but nature's that was causing the disturbance. We had hit particularly rough seas. The ship was going back and forth like a metronome.

Seasickness is one thing they never show you in the commercials.

When you're on a boat, however, that's your whole world. If it's tossing and turning like an insomniac, so are you. There isn't a damn thing you can do about it. You're like a BB in a blender. When I went in search of medical aid, I stopped in the bathroom, taken aback by what was on display.

There were women in there, dressed to go shopping on Worth Avenue, vomiting their brains out with such gusto that I'm sure the strain did more for their complexions than an oil drum full of Retin-A ever could have.

And to think, the night before we had seen a PR extravaganza for the cruise line that promised, through that famous Queen song, "We will rock you." Who'd have thought it was an out-and-out threat?

A handful of seasickness pills made the whole thing quite a bit easier, though traveling this way has a few drawbacks. There is a strange feeling of confinement, even on a ship as big as Rhode Island, that causes the gilded-cage syndrome, opportunity all around and no place to go. They also make the journey from city to city imperceptible. Maybe I'm greedy, but I like to perceive things. A destination without a journey is like an orgasm with no foreplay. Getting there really is half the fun.

But cruises do offer a big picture of coastlines,

like Miami's, and after spending six months snowed into an office building, maybe not perceiving anything more than exactly where the drink boy is at a particular moment really is the best way to go. If opportunity knocked I'd do it again.

The Disney cruise

The Disney cruise" used to mean the glances exchanged by the waiter at Pinocchio's Tavern and the guy playing Pinocchio.

Now it's a ship, and a drop-dead gorgeous one, which I couldn't wait to get on. Disney goes to huge lengths to please, and I longed for their private Bahamian island where nothing bad would happen because Disney wouldn't let it. Fire wouldn't dare break out, nor storm impede, unless they wanted their naturally disasterous asses bought out, merged and quietly extinguished.

My luggage wasn't in our comfortable stateroom as promised. After reporting it I got on deck in time to hear the horn play "When you Wish Upon a Star," at decibel levels I'm surprised didn't send older passengers overboard, clutching their hearts, thinking the world had just ended. I described the bag poorly (it was borrowed) but even untagged luggage was finding its owners, so I waited by the pool in denim shorts and a bra, tattoo exposed, beer in one hand, cigarette in the other, looking like the spokesmodel for white trash but determined not to miss out for lack of apropos swimwear. Still I had a gut feeling as heavy as an anchor that my luggage didn't make it aboard.

I screw up a lot, so I know screw-ups happen. Many staffers were warm and empathic, which makes it easier to be stuck in the Atlantic with only the clothes on your back. But, then one manager described the situation for another who had to comp me the clothes this foul-up had left me without. She began, "Miss Langley has lost her luggage . . . "

Stop, I said. I didn't lose my luggage. You lost my luggage. If you ran a tape of the Tour De France in reverse you wouldn't see anyone backpedal like that girl did. This sneaky spin made my eyes narrow and it was hard to widen them again, despite the scenery.

They gave me a high dollar limit, but the ship store prices were inflated like a 100-man raft, and cheaper items were Golden Girls clothes you'd have to be that old and blind to wear. Then there was panties. I told the girl I'd need a size 7 and she returned with these grandma drawers the size of pillow cases. "I know," said this poor, embarrassed clerk, "they're the only kind we sell." If I hung one of these bloomers over the rail against the wind I could have made the ship turn in circles for hours.

The next day I found neither the hotel nor the port had been checked to see if the bags ever left. Stress multiplying, I now needed this private island, Castaway Cay.

It was stunning, and its best feature was the adult beach, no kitch, no kids, just glowing turquoise water and total silence, a lily free of gilt (Disney owns it but can't fairly get design credit.) After that, dinner and soothing cocktails aboard ship, I accepted that my bag might be lost forever, and that I had failed to lie about its contents: "My home dialysis kit was in that bag!" (grab sides; groan; fall down). I was tan and tired enough not to care.

Til the next day.

After being awakened at 6 AM by announcements, finding $34 overcharges on my bill, enduring a showing of *Up Periscope* on the luxurious bus and then being asked if I saw the luggage go on the truck, like that was my job, I lost it (again) at the Polynesian. There, cruise and hotel staff got on the case like piranha swimming in caffeinated water. Inside of an hour they found out my bag had never left the port, news I had waited two days to hear. I don't know who was happier, them to see me leave or me to get into my own underwear.

Look. Things happen. Luggage gets lost all the time. I have no doubt these kinks will be worked out and the Disney Cruise line will succeed breezily. The Disney Magic is, for the company, the ability to make everything they touch turn to gold. But to me, it will always include their mysterious ability to make my luggage disappear.

Is it cramped in here, or am I crazy?

One of the pictures you are bound to see in the 1997 year-end issue of every magazine you pick up, is that of alleged Unabomber Theodore Kaczynski's tiny home being hauled on a flatbed truck from its original place in the Montana woods through the streets of Sacramento. Though he has refused to undergo psychiatric evaluation, which could be considered a fairly shrewd move for an alleged loony, his defense attorneys plan to use his cabin and its contents to show that the former math professor is as mad as a Hatter and not responsible for his actions.

There is no way Ted is in full possession of his marbles. Sane people make cookies or money or passes at sexy folks, not bombs from scratch. On the other hand, it's kind of interesting that a person's lifestyle can be literally dragged into a courtroom and used as evidence that they're out of their mind. That Kaczynski was able to live for more than 20 years without electricity and only a wood burning stove to stave off the Montana cold is supposed to prove that he's stark raving bonkers. Also, it was pointed out in a Reuter's news story that three door locks were visible on the cabin door, a detail that helps indicate he is paranoid schizophrenic, and therefore unable to formulate the intent to kill. My own mother has three locks on her front door and has done without air-conditioning in Florida for more than 20 years, and while she acts like one of Nurse Ratched's patients sometimes I'm pretty sure that she's not a mental case and is in full possession of the ability to form intent to kill, or at least make you feel really, really guilty, and is therefore sane.

Still, I wish they would conduct every case in the world this way and I got to be on every jury. Imagine how much fun it would be to have the bailiff hand you a big rubber stamp that says "Wack Job," and set you loose in someone else's house and you got to rummage through all their stuff, picking out the items or features you thought made them especially loopy and then stamping them with your court-approved opinion. Stamping things and judging people are both fun activities and you would get to do them together. Say you find a tell-tale price tag. What? The defendant paid $300 for a pair of shoes? WACK JOB. Store-bought copy of the First Wives Club? WACK JOB. Perot for President button? WACK JOB. Kids? On his salary? That's crazy. WACK JOB (stamp the kids). And that wife. Who would marry her? WACK JOB. You get the picture.

In fact, I can't think of anyone I know whose house or apartment, if hauled away to the courthouse on the

back of a big truck, to be inspected by a team of psychol-
ogists, would not yield up one piece of evidence that
called their sanity to be speculated upon with a big fat
question mark. In fact, here is a list of possessions that
are or were in the hands or homes of people that I know
that I believe would make any shrink worth his or her
diploma scribble furiously, with furrowed brow, into their
notebooks:

Cremated remains kept in lunch box, no call
waiting, partial real adult human skeleton, firearms,
full-sized refrigerator in middle of living room, pictures of girls with unlit cigarettes where cigarettes
ought never be placed, elaborate systems of strings,
pulleys and fishing sinkers just to turn on a light, intact lamprey (prehistoric sucker-mouthed eel)
preserved in formaldehyde in refrigerator, picture of
self dressed as June Carter Cash, a Beta VCR, wild
woodpecker living in home, a set of found dentures,
and a prized photograph of a beloved pet monkey that
was subsequently killed and eaten by members of a
neighboring village. No kidding. (Two of the items
listed, by the way, belong to me. If you can identify
which ones they are, and I don't know you, I'll send
you an Orlando Weekly Music Awards t-shirt, if we
have any left*).

Nothing so sinister as bomb-making
instructions, but any of them could be viewed with
suspicion. Surely there are piles of evidence that could
help either side prove Kaczynski's guilt or craziness
that they don't have to resort to putting his way of life

*answers at end of text

158

on trial. The tactic of proving his madness by his cramped, isolated, primitive way of life has been called the "Thoreau defense," after Henry David Thoreau, who looked at society in 1854, said "Screw this," and went off to live on his own in the woods. He is now required reading in school, crazy or not. Ted Kaczynski had the kind of lifestyle that would have been written of glowingly in *Utne*, had it not included blowing people to smithereens, so the germ of evil has to be there, the place it grows in is incidental. If you tried to prove an Amish person crazy for being a primitive loner, you'd have a problem on your hands. The acts committed in this case were indefensible. But not wanting to live like everyone else shouldn't have to be defended.

This coming from a person who, for all you know, had a monkey who got eaten for dinner.

The actual answers to this quiz were a) cremated remains in lunch box; and b) intact lamprey (prehistoric sucker-mouthed eel) preserved in formaldehyde in refrigerator. Fortunately for my mailing bill, only two t-shirts commemorating the Orlando Weekly Music Awards were sent out as only two persons came even close to guessing that these items belonged to me. Unfortunately, and perhaps a little frighteningly, there was a real spike upward in the number of people who believed that I am the type of person who would dress up as June Carter Cash and have my picture taken. I am not sure what this says about me and have not had the nerve to give it any real consideration.

Overstating their impotence

Clean sheets, sugar, vibrating underwear, stronger glasses, you name it, if it makes life better, I think you should have it. The pursuit of happiness is our Constitutional right and it would be traitorous not to jump for joy and its ingredients. Anyway, the more fun everyone has the better off we all are. Happy people don't flip you off in traffic. They don't scream at their kids in the mall, they don't get defensive and they mind their own business because business is good. Happiness is exponential. And since a low quality sex life is a banana peel on the road to happiness, I'll support whatever healthful thing helps squeak the bedsprings of my fellow Americans.

The one thing that makes life easier by making it harder is Viagra, which, as a patriotic hedonist, I have to champion. I think it's great that old people will get to have more sex. Maybe it will keep them off the road. Codger ennui will be a thing of the past, since getting up in the morning is a good reason to get up in the morning. I don't know where Viagra comes from, they may have just stuck a tap in Bill Clinton. Word is that Bob Dole has a prescription. If I were Liddy I'd schedule a Red Cross trip that would take 20 years, to Mars, maybe.

And it's not just old guys. Even not-so-old guys find their car stuck at the bottom of the roller coaster sometimes. It's not the end of the world, but it makes them feel depressed, angry, insecure, guilty and hurt. That's no damn good. They have the right to pursue happiness, and if their happiness is pursuit, well, hurrah for Mr. Frisky. Who would want to deprive anyone of a confident sex life?

The answer is some folks in the insurance industry, but only if you're a woman.

Viagra has only been out for a month and in that time a record-setting 570,000 prescriptions have been written for it. Over half of those were paid in cash, but insurance companies are already including the drug in their regular plans. By contrast, only one-third of policies pay for women's birth control which has been prescribed since the 1960's. Birth control coverage is offered, but additional premiums are usually required. In other words, men are getting erections for free and women are paying for them.

The fear of pregnancy provokes the same dark feelings (depression, anger, etc.) as impotence does. And a pregnancy invariably costs the woman, the insurer, maybe even the country more money than a packet of pills would have. But assuring women of the same confident sex life that's encouraged for men is too much to ask. After all, we're just women. Who cares if we're healthy and happy? As long as fellas got their groove back for cheap, we'll go on trying to pay for all the kids their newfound spring will create. As long as they're hard, who cares if we're hard up?

The limp thinking that created this imbalance seems to come from sources like Deacon Frank Clark of the Catholic Archdiocese of Philadelphia who said "The pill helps men do something they should be able to normally but can't because of a medical condition. . . . Pregnancy isn't a medical condition; it's completely normal."

I've done plenty of whining about the sappy, tyrannous image of pregnancy-cum-sainthood and will agree that reproduction is just biology. But if having a creature growing inside you is not a medical condition, I'm stumped as to what is. But there you go, a Catholic church rep says pregnancy is no biggie (unless you want to abort, in which case it's a miracle and you're on a greased poll to hell). Pregnant women will be glad to know it's not a medical condition. Cancel your sonogram and have a tequila shooter, you're probably just in a mood. If it isn't medical, perhaps it's just a design flaw. The imperfection clearly is that you were not born a man.

The inequity is summed up neatly in *The Witches of Eastwick*, when Devil explains the Salem witch hunts: "[Men are] scared. Their dicks get limp when confronted by a woman of obvious power and what do they do about it? Call them witches, burn them, torture them, until every woman is afraid. Afraid of herself, afraid of men. And all for what? Fear of losing their hard-ons."

It would go a long way to explain why, in this century, women fear for their lives in going to certain clinics while men are putting on party hats to celebrate the awakening of Rip Van Winkus.

Okay, I do know how Viagra works. It increases blood flow to the affected region and makes it function. If there was such a pill that worked on the brain, these inequities would cease. For now, the brain, the womb, the unplanned children, everything will have to wait in line behind the penis, the MVP. Typically, I'd be head cheerleader at Uncle Wiggly's pep rally, and I'd never be so miserly as to suggest that Viagra not be covered by insurance (but I think air conditioning, swimming pools and good wine should be covered, too; they do promote better health). But since they're making us take sides, I'm on the girl's team, and until birth control coverage is mandatory, we're getting screwed.

And picking up the tab for it, to boot.

Where the boys aren't

The late legitimate egghead and intellectual darling Joseph Campbell once explained mankind's climb out of the animal rut by pointing to the first found artifact that was not useful but simply artistic. This, he said, showed more than just a desire to survive, but a need for truth and beauty. It's the difference between being animal and being human.

It's also the difference between the bachelor party and the bridal shower.

Everyone knows what goes on at the idiot hit parade known as the bachelor party. Bachelor parties are when men congregate to get stinking drunk, hit on women with Zoto perms and sometimes just get tattooed.

Bridal showers, on the other hand, are ordered, mannerly affairs with more rituals than Catholicism and more civility than may be contained in the subsequent marriage. They are that difference between animal and human: They are not about going berserk and snorting one another out like pigs hunting truffles; they are about reaching for something better, something higher, something wrapped in silver paper that you yourself could never afford. They are about presents.

And other things: celebrating, being happy for the bride, drinking champagne cocktails . . . and unwrapping the presents.

Showers, bridal or baby, have always been curious rituals to men. They are also an alien world to some women, women who saw *Snow White* as girls but didn't start wishing for Prince Charming; instead we wished that we, too, could hand someone we hated a shiny red apple and watch that person fall over like a sack of potatoes. Girlie though we are, proper notions of romance winged past our heads like bullets in the desert. (We know we heard something, but we just kept walking.)

Carolyn, though, is a girl who knows the rules, and Carolyn is getting married. She is our friend and a Lady, and we do wish her well, did get that cocktail, did bear gifts and now, having seen the inner workings of that ceremony that is the bridal shower, we'd like to tell you about it.

Arrival: There are jobs to do at a bridal shower, all revolving around the presents. They will not start opening them without you if they expect you to bring one. Still, it's okay to arrive a bit late, because that gives everyone time to knock a couple back and get a little silly, because everyone will feel silly by the time these rituals commence anyway.

Presents: Bridal shower gifts should be either practical (an IUD) or romantic (the "Bride and

Groom" champagne glasses from your failed marriage) or sexy lingerie (which is both).

Rules: there are some practical rules to bridal showers, like how one person is supposed to take the names of everyone who has given anything. This is the bride's thank-you note list. (A keen observer noted that the hostess should just have a stack of cards sitting right there and the bride could just sign them and hand them out, saving everyone time and stamps.)

A shower superstition is that each ribbon or bow the bride breaks is also the number of children that will come from the marriage. This is a stupid idea: It dooms careful brides to barrenness and clumsy ones to a life as the old woman who lived in a shoe. Besides, everyone knows that you can break all the ribbons in the world and remain safe, but if you suspect anything latex has snapped, then you've got problems.

A bridal shower idea of cute is for someone to write down everything the bride says when she opens stuff and repeat the list back later; supposedly that's what she's going to say on her wedding night. You are expected to find remarks like "Oh, I love it,"and "Oh, it's so big," etc. Sweet, eh?

Hopefully she will outsmart you and say things like, "Well that's sort of lifelike" and, "Oh. I already have one of those."

Lastly, someone is supposed to take all those ribbons and stick them together. This clump of festivity then masquerades as the bridal bouquet at the wedding rehearsal, where the bride practices for the day she throws actual flowers at someone who is then supposed to get married so we can all do the whole thing over again. This, as far as we could see, was the end to the formal bridal shower ceremony, and the point at which everyone breaks for booze, cake and conversation as God intended.

Considering it in retrospect, the bridal shower is just like the wedding, without the judge/priest/offici-ator, stupid overdone taffeta and legal commitment. So it really is true and beautiful after all!

An ill wind in the willows

It's a wonderful day for a protest. The air is smartly cool, even cold, and the sunshine seems to have been buffed to an extra high gloss for the occasion. An orgasm of flowers is spilling over the grounds around Cinderella's castle in the Magic Kingdom, but there is no time to wallow in this sweetness.

After getting lost within Disney's sprawling estate I am already late for the event. With radicals, you can never tell: Will they throw frog's blood all over the building? Occupy the Hall? Capture Pooh bear and shove bamboo up his honey pot? Acts of rebellion happen as fast as an out-of-control motorcar. I race to the appointed protest sight expecting mayhem, smoke and banners swaying in the wind. What I find is six people standing demurely in green T-shirts. These are terrorists who could be mistaken for people deciding where to eat.

This is the scene, or lack of it, in front of Mr. Toad's Wild Ride, which rumor says will be euthanized like a family dog that's just gotten too old to be fun anymore, and replaced by the more popular Winnie the Pooh and his Hundred-Acre Wood. The speculation led young South Floridian Jef Moskot to build a website, where hundreds have left toadying messages in support of their beloved frog (originally brought to life in Kenneth Grahame's 1908 novel *The Wind in the Willows*, and to cartoon glory by Disney in 1949) who they feel has been sorely neglected.

There is no Toad walking around in a character suit, no Toad merchandise, and although a recent live-action film of the classic, starring members of Monty Python, enjoyed lavish praise from *The New York Times*, it was only released in three cities. And as we all know, we're up to our eyeballs in Pooh.

Recently, the webbed Toads called for "a stop to this villainy" by urging fans to gather in front of the ride on a particular Sunday earlier this month. The turnout is disappointing.

"There are some non-shirted people here who are afraid to wear [the shirts]. They work in 'themed entertainment,'" says Jennifer Mandelion, speaking in spy code and wearing one of the green shirts with a cartoon of a dead Toad on the front and the come-on, "Ask Me Why Mickey is Killing Mr. Toad," on the back. (Despite her frog-kissing affiliation, she wears a Pooh wrist watch.) The cowardly collaborators are seated at tables across from the ride, watching their valiant brothers fight the amphibious fight. As for Disney's official position, which has been not to come out and say directly that there will be frog's legs for dinner, "I think it's a done deal," she says. "We've heard rumors that the honey pots are already being worked on."

The Toadies confide that there are Disney "suits" all around, monitoring their behavior, and they are afraid they will be toad away. Sure enough, as soon as a passing vacationer approaches them (as many do; lots of park guests saw the news and feel compelled to take what could be their last Wild Ride) and is handed a flyer, two park officials intervene, albeit pleasantly, and say no literature can be passed out, and then tell me that I must be accompanied by a press representative in order to work in the park. When I reply that my calls to the press office were never returned and that I paid to get in, I seem to be off the hook. I realized the Toadies are right; like a clumsy and obvious FBI, there seem to be more suits and wires than there are toad activists.

Moskot says he loves the toad because "the lead character is as insane as I am" (the story, you may recall, centers on Toad's compulsive, impassioned behavior, which gets him in trouble), and the group echoes the website's admissions of sadness at another piece of the original park being removed. Out of the corner of my ear I hear Karen, who has come all the way from Peterborough, Ontario, to attend a Disney fan gathering (the toad protest just happened to take place at the same time), say that she is "a toad virgin." She has never even ridden the ride before, yet risks being deported to the real world to stand in its favor.

It's time she went on the ride.

Since I was wrong about a mob of international camera crews covering the event and am, in fact, the only reporter who turned out, I ride the ride along with its defenders. They insist that Karen's first exposure should be through the "naked lady" entrance, referring to one of the cartoon images. People in line ask about the cause; Jef says one who approached him was upset that this wasn't "a real controversy," expecting, perhaps, to hear about corruption or sweatshops, and pissed that it was only about a ride. Karen wants to sit with Jef. "I should lose my toad . . . in the company of someone who knows what they're doing."

On the ride, the toadsters do not jump out of the car and chain themselves to the toad-embossed andirons. They behave just as you want people you're on rides with to behave. They scream, they point at things with enthusiasm ("Naked Lady!" "Weasels!" "Satan!") and shout, "We're all gonna die!" They are happy. But at our exit we are greeted by a Suit, an attractions manager who approaches the group. The team is wary. Will he give them the boot? Have they gone too far? Have they poisoned the minds of heretofore unblemished park-goers with their subversive shirts? "If you'd like to go and ride the other side, too, I'll take you through. You won't have to wait in line," he says. We are getting a police escort through the gates of victory. But isn't that what the capitalist running dogs always do, ply the enemy with hospitality and cake, and then take them someplace where they are never heard from again? Mysteriously, this time, our safety bar doesn't lower; we get stuck several times, with the Weasels, with the phantom train. The group had said earlier that there are rumors of "secret rooms" inside the ride, filled with "cool stuff." But are they really filled with cells where the enemies of the people are chloroformed and locked up? Alas, no. Once again we go through hell and back, unscathed.

Karen likes this side even better. "It was more worth it than I ever expected," she says, more than most virgins can boast. The group is exhilarated and happy as we part company. Twenty minutes later they are gone altogether. They have a lot more of Disney to wallow in before returning to their respective homes in Florida, Texas, New York and Canada. Even the most strident dissidents have to have a little fun. Toadally.

(On September 7, 1998, "Toad" croaked. Oh, pooh.)

Feeling a little cocky

What song is stuck in your head right now?

Be honest. You know there's some tune bopping around in there all the time, and it's never your favorite. You may have heard a snatch of "Dirty White Boy," and now you're stuck with it. But that's OK. Whatever song it is, it's not a fraction as humiliating as what's simpering through my synapses, which is "The Penis Song" from *Monty Python's The Meaning of Life.*

"Isn't it awfully good to have a penis? Isn't it frightfully good to own a dong?"

Try living with that all day and the fear of absent-mindedly crooning it aloud while you're pumping gas.

Not that I would know what a big, honking thrill it is to look down and have Mr. Clean winking up at me all the time. That's the point. The reason for my mental soundtrack is because I'm reading *Dick for a Day*, a 1997 book that asked 54 women writers, "What would you like to do if, by some mysterious means, you had a penis for one day?"

It isn't intended to promote penis envy, says editor Fiona Giles. It's Exploration, not thievery, that she was after, to get women to think long and hard about this thing that is at once so close and so alien to them—not to belittle men, but to imagine life in their underwear.

Under wraps

For me, *Dick* was that gigantic, shiny Christmas present with my name on it. You don't want to rip it open right away. You want to hold it up to your ear and shake it first (the book, not the newfound penis), to hold the anticipation in your hands. In other words, as a woman, it's impossible to even open this book before fantasizing about what you would do with a chance to "hijack maleness," in spirit and form, for 24 hours.

Just to be one of those annoying people who unwraps presents one piece of tape at a time, we'll talk spirit first and save flesh for later. Female is a lush, lavish, velvety way to live. But I think it would be great to be a man. I'd like to walk—alone—at night, anywhere, and never be afraid. I'd like to get seriously pissed off and not have anyone whisper "period." I'd like to get out of this Victoria's Secret straightjacket. I think it'd be great to have bigness be a source of swagger. And to have someone look at you with auto-matic confidence that you can fix the car and every-thing else in the whole world.

So, now that the wrapper is off, it's time to dive into the actual package, and the first thing is thinking about what kind of package you'd have. Mine would be huge. Absolute Gigantor. Something you could give someone a shiner with. No nonsense about aesthetics or proportion, this is my only shot at the three-legged race, and I want a Foster's oil can. Nonetheless, for the sake of continuity, it would be white.

OK, then, what does anyone do with a new toy? In my scant 24 hours I'd forego food, drink and sleep, and play with it till I was a hair's breath from hospitalization, an exhausted and happy slave of the white whale. Call me Ahab. I might share the wealth, if there was time. It's hard to say. If I kept my own body I'd try to make the cover of *Chicks with Dicks*.

Male prerogatives

Some of the women's answers in the book were similar, but some were so thoughtful that my shallow flippancy was embarrassing. Marissa Acocella said she would give a woman as many orgasms as she could to make up for ones she never had. Germaine Greer would donate to a sperm bank. Pat Califa wrote about the poor way society treats men, especially gay ones, right before she ripped into a fantasy about prowling gay-male leather bars. Carol Wolper talked about how she'd watch a woman at lunch eat two bites of lettuce, going away hungry and wired, while Wolper her/himself, "well-fed and pumped," then would pass some thin compliment to the woman, watching her eyes light up and thinking, "This stuff is so easy it's criminal."

After reading what others had to say I repeated the original make-believe experiment. Whenever a question, funk or dilemma faced me, instead of quietly taking it in, I imagined that I'd face it back, pointing at it with my extroverted ghost totem. This made me giggle in a way that would make the other guys knock the snot out of me. But it made every decision a snap. It turned "What if I'm wrong?" into "Eh, who cares?" This sudden clarity could have been just the result of playing pretend, or it could be the side effect of the sureness I project onto male shoulders. All that matters, though, is the result (isn't that a Machiavellian, male thing to think?) and putting a loud exclamation point where once were whispering parentheses placed everything in auto-focus.

This probably proves that I'd be exactly the kind of shallow, self-absorbed dork that women always accuse penis-possessors of being. If I had a dick, there's every chance in the world I'd be one. Maybe. Just for a day.

Working It Out

Once my friend Bob and I went gambling in Biloxi. Miss Bob sat there with a fez-sized cup full of nickels, cramming them into a slot machine to no result, when the old lady on the next stool began kibitzing. She looked more like a Wal-Mart regular than Diamond Jane Brady, but that didn't stop her from ragging on him, as if his evaporating nickels didn't speak loud and clear. Bob whispered, "That's the first time since fifth grade I've been yelled at for not winning."

It was one of those understated mouthfuls and it made me realize how lucky we were to be grown up. Parents tell kids they're living the best years of their lives. Parents lie. Compared to powerless youth, adulthood kicks ass like Jackie Chan. If you're a kid, just wait till you get here. Many adults are so relieved when they finally arrive that they sleep, in a certain way, through the rest of the show.

Adults have to make rent, but that's nothing. Think of the advantages. As an adult you don't have to be good at geometry, Shakespeare and soccer all in one day unless you want to. Adults don't all know the same things. No one gives us the heavy sigh because we can't all mix a martini, execute a flying scissors kick and dry-clean pants. And mostly, as an adult you'll never, I mean never, find an unsolicited baseball flying at your skull unless you're drinking beer in the stands, or be required to run 600 yards unless something's chasing you, or have someone with a clipboard scream "Rotate!" just before you break your wrist serving a volleyball into the net.

That was P.E., the nightmare it takes 10 years to wake up from. After school we all played everything well enough and happily, but the interrogation-lamp pressure of P.E. could make anyone throw up, something I remember a kid doing after a couple of those endless runs. I recall an archery class in which a friend of mine made a half-assed attempt to William Tell the teacher. The teacher told him, to my recollection, it wasn't funny. Of course not. He had missed.

P.E. made us more than nauseous and homicidal. I place blame for America's mostly Sta-Puft physiques squarely on the shoulders of P.E., which made us roundly hate and avoid all physical exertion, kind of the way lab animals flinch and shrink when they see clipboards and cameras. Anyone who got the full P.E. experience still reacts to the spurt of a whistle like a monkey on a hot plate.

If anyone had told me when I was a Catholic schoolgirl that I would one day take gym voluntarily, I would have screamed for an exorcist. But once out of school you discover sports can be fun and that using your body, even in legal public ways, feels good.

I'm grateful for teachers like Connie Hayes at Paramount Health Club, where I go to get screamed at by women in tights and like it. For one thing, Connie does all the work with you. I never had a P.E. teacher who moved more vigorously than a set of wind chimes. And Connie tells you why you're doing what you're doing. A tough stretch becomes very easy when you're told it will give you a guitar curve. Having someone explain their job by blowing a whistle and pointing to a field—as a way of saying "get out there!"—is discouraging because that's how you communicate with dogs, and dogs don't grade you.

Some radicals are promoting a new way of getting kids worked up: by making the workout fun. *The Wall Street Journal* reported this fall that "the new P.E.," while not widespread, is catching on. At one school kids can watch CNN while pedaling stationary bikes, elect to take a tap-dancing class or play "heart-rate basketball," in which points are awarded for the effort of getting your heart rate above a target level. It beats standing around waiting 40 minutes to run the 50-yard dash, your heart rate increasing only out of dread. At another school, kids play a form of tag that requires a touch from a rubber chicken. Who wouldn't run a half mile if you got to whap someone with a rubber chicken at the end? I want to do that now.

The new P.E. blossomed because students were losing interest in gym and gaining weight. Now, instead of hiding to avoid dodge ball, they're doing yoga and canoeing. This has increased P.E. enrollment at some schools. Cowboys realized that making yourself agreeable to your charge, a la *The Horse Whisperer*, is a more effective and more enduring way of imposing your designs than breaking its spirit. Gym teachers just now seem to be learning that this could apply to children, too.

I wish it had happened 20 years ago. But at least points have been made against calisthenics in the name of students' better health. Finally, someone is blowing the whistle on P.E.

Purple passion

On the eve of the Senate vote over whether to impeach the president, the most talked-about news story in the country was about a guy who got all freaked out because he thinks this one pretend baby space alien's a queer.

The only person who could get their hackles raised over the sexuality of felt is holy roly-poly Jerry Falwell, the preacher who seems happily snuggled up to the deadly sins of gluttony and pride. I have to hand it to him. I thought I was good, but his smut vision is world-class, and he deserves the horny crown as the King of Nudge-Nudge Wink-Wink more than I do.

Falwell, the only guy who could say the Antichrist is going to be a Jew and still keep his job, has announced that one of the Teletubbies is gay. The Teletubbies. The sweet, baby-voiced, gourd-shaped PBS darlings with TVs for tummies who rise to an infant-faced sun and teach us how kids learn. Falwell thinks they have a genital agenda. His twitchy finger points to Tinky Winky. Tinky is purple, the gay-pride color. His antenna is shaped like a triangle, the official symbol of gay pride. And he carries a red vinyl purse.

Right and wrong

How come, if they represent the far right, they're always out in left field? Purpleness and sexual ambiguity don't mean Tinky is gay; they mean he's Prince. Besides, whatever Teletubbies are, their audience is made up of two-year-olds. Two-year-olds are barely aware of what gender is, never mind its bendability. And what Ralph Kramden-era mindset pictures gay men as carrying purses? Gay men don't carry purses, and if they did, they wouldn't carry something as tacky as that red vinyl number of Tinky's.

It's even easier to say, well, duh, of course Tinky Winky's gay. What straight male allows himself to be called Tinky Winky? His belly screen never shows anything but Joan Crawford movies and "Dawson's Creek." A close look reveals wrist bands and hand stamps from all the bars in Teletubby Village. He's the only one of the characters with a gym membership. That purse is a Tommy Hilfiger, and you know what's in it? The Friday classifieds with all the good estate sales circled in red. So Chubby Smugs figured out that Tinky Winky is a Nellie-Tubby. Big deal. My mom could have figured that out, and they didn't even have gay people back when she was young.

Without a doubt Tinky Winky has said nothing but "uh-oh" ever since the outing, and that's not going to help when it's time for his *Genre* interview. He really should get Chastity Bono to help him through this. In the meantime, the rest of us are wondering, what's new? It's not as though children's programming hasn't brought us lots of lovable gay characters in the past.

Bert and Ernie might have separate beds, but so did Lucy and Ricky. Bugs Bunny was squeezing into drag and smooching Elmer Fudd every chance he got. Ren and Stimpy sleep in the same bed, and Stimpy dreams dreamy dreams of mothering Ren's children while Ren is cold and abusive. (Come to think of it, Stimpy doesn't suggest homosexuality so much as battered-wife syndrome.) And that butch Peppermint Patty had her little sidekick Marcie calling her "sir." With that roll call it seems very possible that about 10 percent of the population of Saturday morning cartoons is gay, statistically reflecting the population of the country.

Toy story

How do you even get to a point of such severe delusion that outing dolls is relevant to your spirituality? Compared to the real spirituality of those who don't have their own TV network, the Falwellian spirituality is like fat-free cheese: You can tell yourself it's great because it leaves you guilt- and blame-free, but you know it's not great, it's not even good, and it doesn't come close to being satisfying. We all feel that hunger of the soul, the pang of wanting to know there's something more to this whole mess. Don't tell me you get that itch scratched by looking for erections in *The Little Mermaid* or sex in the stars of *The Lion King*.

Maybe Falwell was just jealous because the Teletubbies' creators are making such big piles of money without having to threaten anybody with the jaws of hell. Maybe, since they seem unable to get anybody riled up anymore over abortion or teaching evolution, the Christian soldiers just needed to find something else to shoot at.

You'd think they'd have learned from the whole Clinton affair, though, that people don't really care for hatefulness and dirt-digging, and most probably couldn't care less whether one or all of the Teletubbies are gay. Most people don't waste time saying "uh-oh" over and over, whether there is anything to uh-oh about or not.

A woman's touch

I have never overheard anyone having sex. My friends have, but I myself have never been subjected to the moans, sighs and squeaking springs that suggest some couple in the next room has just moved seven inches closer to God.

This lack of evidence doesn't prevent me from being nervous about being overheard myself. You'd think I would have had more reason to be nervous when I was dating. But in the absence of a boyfriend, it's the telltale buzz from my apartment that I fear cuts through the walls. I wonder if my neighbors think I have a carpentry shop in my room, or that I'm a caterer, Cuisinarting for wedding parties and bar mitzvah crowds. Maybe they think I raise hornets.

I'm pretty sure I'm not single-handedly keeping the vibrator industry in business, but I can't say for sure; vibrators are something no one ever talks about. And while I understand the taboo, I owe that device more gratitude than embarrassment. My appreciation increased when I realized how easily it could be taken away from me if I lived in Alabama. A state law passed there last year prohibits the sale of vibrators and other "harmful" sex toys under penalty of a

$10,000 fine and a year in jail or "hard labor." That's some interpretation of "penal code."

Oh (Big) Brother

Fourteen other states have similar laws but, according to a report by ABC News, most don't enforce them. Alabama is right on our doorstep and I find it upsetting that our neighbors are subjected to this kind of Orwellian idiocy. "Why?" is the most obvious question, and the most obvious answer is that some legislators have pens that are mightier than their personal swords, and the idea that women can satisfy themselves is emasculating and intolerable to them. That may be getting a little personal, but so is telling people how they can masturbate.

Which brings up the law's screamingly sexist nature. It's impossible to prohibit the use of male self-stimulators, unless the state decides to go Iranian and cut off the hand that commits the crime. If that happened you'd probably see some Alabama legislators looking like Luke Skywalker after he found out who his daddy was. Let's not forget, too, that while this attempt is being made to curtail the sexual satisfaction of women, the male sex aid Viagra was practically greeted with ticker-tape parades. Science lends men a helping hand while government takes one away from women.

It's the sale of vibrators, not their use, that is made illegal through this law, which has come to light because six Alabama women are suing the state for violating their privacy rights. But you can't use one if you can't first buy one; nobody gives vibrators away like promotional pens (although it would be great to get a free one that says "Craftsman Tool Club" on the side of it every time you apply for a Sears charge card). So if anyone is setting up a smuggling operation to bring the much-needed devices to our sisters in the Lobotomy State, count me in. ABC says that even in China the sale of vibrators is state-approved by the Beijing Family Planning Commission, with the items available for purchase at a state hospital sex shop. Sex therapists know that vibrators can be and have been helpful for more than 100 years.

I don't want to be the spokesmodel for Good Vibrations (maybe "hand model" would be a better term), but they do nothing but good. They're cheaper than therapy, easier to set up than an iMac and they're idiot-proof: As long as you're not sticking them up your nose, your satisfaction is guaranteed.

Replaceable you

And they could save your life. Single people whose hormones have gathered enough strength to whip a house into a tree frequently settle for company that would be unacceptable at any other time. If you can feed yourself, you can hold back for the main course; if you're starving, you're going to grab the first stale cracker you find lying around.

Maybe even one from Alabama.

Yes, there are some things an actual human being can offer that a machine can't. A machine isn't much fun to curl up next to, and you can't give anything back to it, which is half the fun.

But the vibe has some perks humans don't have. It's got no family and no past. It's going to be there for you, because it lives in the drawer. There's never any need for debate; it's get-in-and-get-out, like an efficient shopper. And if you don't like it anymore you can throw it out the window.

The most keen-eyed observation on the Alabama law comes from Bill Winter, director of communications for the Libertarian Party, who said that his group suspects "the thrill people get from sex toys is nothing compared to the thrill politicians get from controlling other people's lives."

Hear, hear. Just don't do it outside my door.